ELEVATING YOUR PATIENT EXPERIENCE

from Ordinary *to* Exceptional

ELEVATING YOUR PATIENT EXPERIENCE

HOW TO GO BEYOND SERVICE AND SATISFACTION BY CREATING MORE HAPPINESS, HIGHER REVENUE, AND BETTER RESULTS

from Ordinary *to* Exceptional

JEAN-PAUL BRUTUS, MD

Elevating Your Patient Experience from Ordinary to Exceptional

Copyright © 2023 Jean-Paul Brutus, MD

All rights reserved. No part of this book may be reproduced or used in any manner without written permission of the copyright owner except for the use of quotations in a book review.

First edition 2023

Published by Exception MD Publishing, exceptionmd.ca

Jean-Paul Brutus, drbrutus.com

ISBN: 978-1-7775361-5-2 (English hardcover)

ISBN: 978-1-7775361-6-9 (English eBook)

ISBN: 978-1-7775361-8-3 (English paperback)

ISBN: 978-1-7775361-7-6 (English audiobook)

Book consulting by Stanley Dankoski of The Grounded Writer
www.groundedwriter.com

Cover design and interior layout by Becky's Graphic Design®, LLC
www.beckysgraphicdesign.com

Photos of author and Exception MD by Bassam Sabbagh of Kurious Photography, Montreal, Quebec, Canada
www.kuriousphoto.com

All other photos purchased from Adobe Stock.

Real patient feedback included in this book have been edited for brevity and clarity.

To my beautiful wife, Stephanie,

my furry son, Mr. Alfie, and Edgar the cat.

Without your love and support, nothing is possible.

This book would certainly not have been.

To all patients around the world, who deserve the most beautiful experience of care the community of physicians and other healers can offer.

Table of Contents

Introduction ... 1

PART I The Current Patient Experience

1. Why Do You Care? ... 7
2. Who Will Benefit Most from This Book and Why ... 17
3. The Burdens of the Status Quo ... 27
4. Redefining Patient Experience ... 37
5. How Patients Will Feel in Your Presence ... 49
6. You're Already Providing an Experience ... 55
7. The Infinite Game and a Just Cause ... 61

PART II Creating Exceptional Patient Experiences

8. Start by Asking Questions ... 67
9. Principles of an Exceptional Patient Experience ... 75
10. Create an Exceptional Patient Experience Program ... 87
11. Understand Your Patient's Journey ... 97
12. Identify Your Ideal Patient's Needs and Preferences ... 103
13. Optimize Onboarding of Your Ideal Patient ... 109
14. Design a Facility for Relaxation and Healing ... 115
15. Develop Exceptional Communication Skills and Personalized Care ... 121
16. Elevate Patient Expectations ... 129
17. Optimize the Physical Exam ... 139
18. Elevate the Diagnostic and Surgical Experiences ... 145

PART III Important Tips for Creating Exceptional Patient Experiences

19. Make Lasting Impressions by Creating Memorable Moments and Stories ... 155
20. Resolve Issues with an Exceptional Service Recovery Plan ... 161
21. How NOT to Create an Exceptional Experience ... 165
22. Prevent Burnout, Restore Joy, and Find Fulfillment ... 173

Conclusion ... 177
Acknowledgments ... 183
About the Author ... 185
Other Books by Dr. Jean-Paul Brutus ... 189

Introduction

The concept of creating an exceptional patient experience is important not just to the well-being of the patients themselves, but to the healthcare professionals who provide that care. You may be among the surgeons, physicians, and providers who recognize that more can be done across the board to ease patient fears, smooth the overall process, and meet their needs every step of the way so that they are happy before, during, and after their encounter with you.

Or you may be a healthcare professional who may not fully understand how the scope of the patient experience can impact their impressions of you, their recovery time, and frankly your effectiveness as a trusted provider.

Creating an exceptional patient experience is so important that I had to write this book about it, for the benefit of the healthcare provider.

The journey that led me to write it was born out of pain.

My career plan was to become an academic plastic surgeon specializing in hand surgery. After fifteen years of training, I achieved that goal and began my practice in one of the largest university healthcare centers in Canada.

The Montreal University Hospital Center had about seventeen plastic surgeons in the Department of Plastic and Reconstructive Surgery, and I was hired to be one of the leaders of the Hand Surgery Department.

I had landed my dream job and started my practice at the age of thirty-four. I wanted to help patients who needed complex hand and wrist surgery, use the most advanced and least invasive surgical techniques, teach the hand surgeons of tomorrow, and push the boundaries of modern science by researching, publishing, and presenting my findings around the world. It was my dream job!

But after a few years, I started to feel different. I was always running, working at four different university affiliated hospitals, sitting on too many committees, attending too many early and late teaching meetings, fighting with the administration to get hospital beds or operating room time to operate on my patients. Not to mention being on call too much. I could not get the surgical equipment I needed, and I did not have the resources (human and financial) to support my mission.

Then I asked myself a question that would change my life forever:

Would I want to be a patient under my own care in my hospital?

The honest answer was a painful no.

And the reason was that I didn't think the patient experience I was giving my patients was what I thought it should be.

Patients were waiting too long to see me (often more than six months). They needed a referral from their family doctor in order to see me, even though many of them did not even have a primary care physician.

The pressure to see patients was so great (too many patients, not enough specialists) that I was forced to see anywhere from sixty to ninety patients in a single day. In an eight-hour day, that would mean seeing a new patient every five or six minutes!

My mind was constantly racing and focused on what I needed to do next instead of being present with the patient in front of me, and on top of that, my patients were not getting the best version of me after waiting so long to see me. I was rushed, irritated, impatient, and always thinking about what was next.

This did not seem fair to my patients or to me. If this was the dream job, I no longer wanted it. It was just too painful, and I saw no way to change it from within the system.

So, I left it. And decided to start the first private hand surgery practice in the country, a country without private insurance to help patients pay for surgery, a country where access to universal and free healthcare is considered a human right.

I did it anyway. Because I believed. I believed that Canadians yearned for a higher standard of care. I believed that Canadians wanted options. I believed they were ready to make their own healthcare decisions, rather than be under the thumb of a paternalistic, outdated system. I believed patients wanted more humanity in the way they were treated. More respect. More empathy and compassion.

I did it because I believed it was my duty to create an alternative that would allow me to want to be my own patient under my own care.

I believed that Canadians should have an amazing experience when they are at their most vulnerable and need someone to take care of them.

I was inspired to integrate the principles of hospitality and wellness (think spa) with healthcare and surgery.

An exceptional patient experience became my cause. I chose "Exception MD" as the name of my clinic to reflect that every patient should be treated as an exception.

INTRODUCTION

I am writing this to share with you—surgeons, physicians, and other healthcare professionals—what I have learned over thirteen years of this journey. I am sharing this with you, people who I assume want to help others feel great and have better healthcare experiences. The more of you who say, "Yes, I want to give my patients (and friends, and families, and everyone, really) an exceptional experience," the closer we will get to creating a world where a better experience is the rule, not the exception.

Are you in?

I hope you find what you are looking for, and more.

Live exceptionally,
Jean-Paul

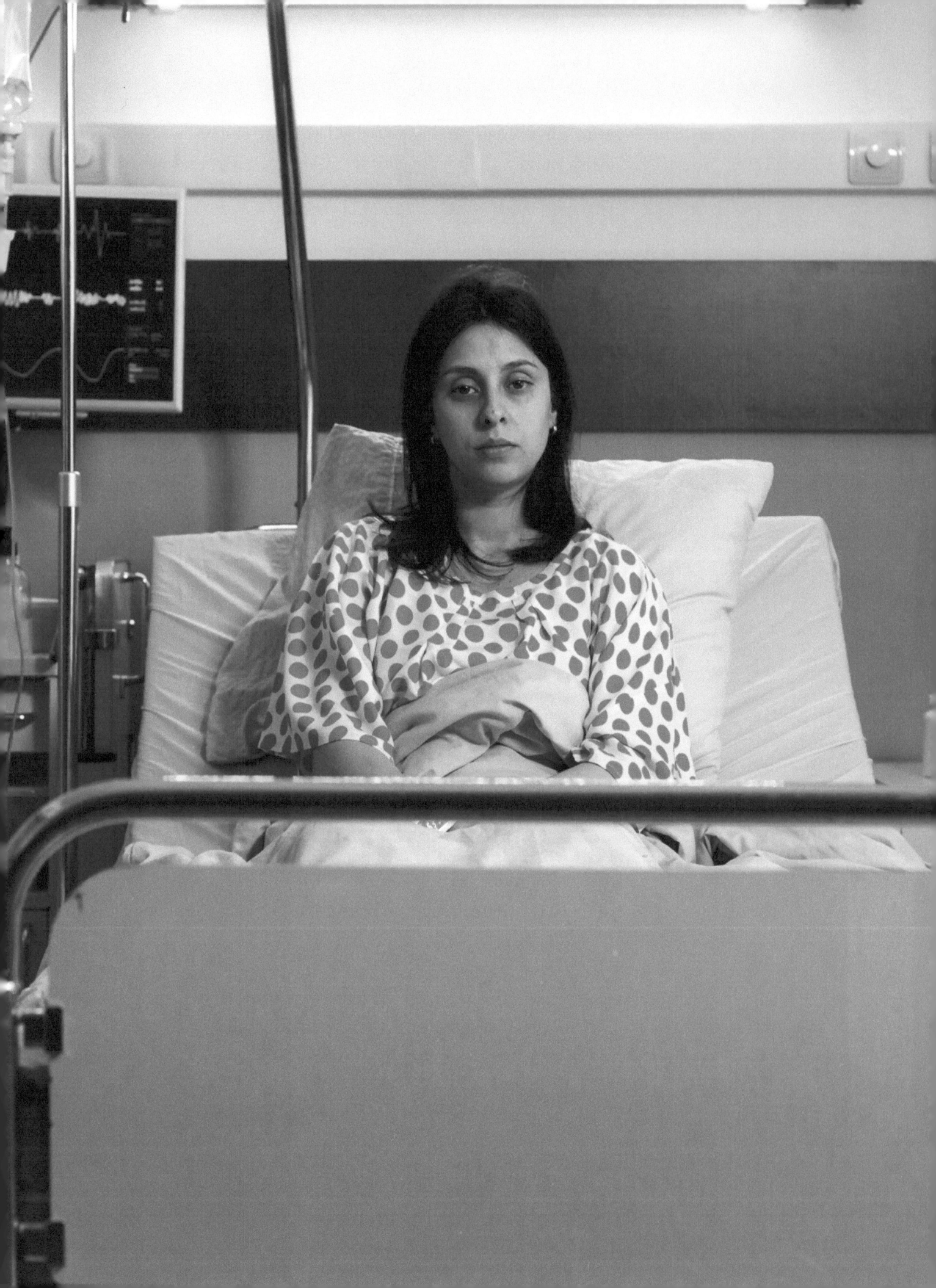

PART 1

The Current Patient Experience

THE CURRENT PATIENT EXPERIENCE

Dr. Brutus is a gifted surgeon. He chose surgery because he wanted to solve people's problems quickly and hands because they are so vital to every aspect of our daily lives.

A nurse from his team followed up with me by phone every morning of the week following the surgery, encouraging care and increasing use of the hand and exercises to help with the healing process. I had one further consultation with Dr. Brutus by Skype ten days after the surgery before he headed out for a well-earned vacation somewhere warm.

I am totally satisfied that the fairly substantial cost of this procedure was well-earned ... and also well-spent compared with waiting a further twelve months in sometimes excruciating pain for the free service available under Medicare.

A sincere thank you to Dr. Brutus and his team.

1

Why Do You Care?

"The way to get started is to quit talking and begin doing."

—WALT DISNEY

I can tell you many reasons why you should care about creating an exceptional patient experience (and, in fact, I will in the next few chapters), but my question for you first is:

Why do YOU care about patient experience?

Why do you care about patients and how they feel at all?

In other words:

Why do you do what you do? And why do you want to do it better?

These questions may seem trivial, but they're not.

WHY you chose WHAT in the way you know HOW

If you want to excel at something, anything, you have to take the time to figure out the real, deep-seated reasons why you want to do it in the first place.

If you don't, you won't commit, you won't give it your all, and you won't develop the discipline to really make a difference. "Dreams without goals are just dreams," Denzel Washington said, "and ultimately they fuel disappointment. On the road to achieving your dreams, you must apply discipline but more importantly consistency, because without commitment, you will never start, but without consistency, you will never finish."

Without the real WHY, you won't start; without the discipline, you won't finish.

Most doctors and healthcare providers are good at describing *what* they do.

This concept is formed in the most advanced, outer layer of your brain, the layer that articulates your thinking: the neocortex. The neocortex is also responsible for language, which is why your WHAT is easiest to describe in words.

In my personal case, after medical school, I trained in plastic surgery and then hand surgery. That is my WHAT:

I change people's lives by operating on their hands.

Describing *how* you do it is also relatively easy, but less so than describing the *what*.

The HOW describes, well, how you do things. In other words, what makes you different from others who do what you do.

My HOW is:

I treat each patient with exceptional personal attention and care, and I operate on them using the least invasive and most innovative surgical techniques.

When I was younger, before I chose a career in medicine, I wanted to go into the hospitality industry. I wanted to be the director of a five-star luxury hotel or resort, like the Ritz Carlton or the Four Seasons.

But in order to do that, I had to go to the best hospitality school in the world, which was in Lausanne, Switzerland. Frankly, at the age of seventeen, I was not ready to move to another country where I knew no one. Besides, the tuition was really high, and I could not afford it.

However, I retained and developed a personal interest and taste for the finest hospitality experiences that these hotels created for their guests, and when I started a private medical practice about twenty years later, I knew that I wanted to integrate the principles of the finest hotel experiences with those of private medicine.

Now you can understand why personalizing the care experience for my patients is so important to me. It goes back a long way.

Understanding the deep and abiding reasons *why* you do what you do and *how* you do it is extremely important because it will drive you forward.

The patient experience you create depends on it. When the going gets tough, it's your WHY that will keep you going. When you are challenged by an anxious patient or family member, living your WHY will make a difference in how you act rather than react. You will better understand what makes you fulfilled and satisfied. Your choices will be more intentional.

The WHY will be your starting point, your present moment, and your destination, all aligned in perfect harmony.

Consider the team you have, or the one you'll need to build, in order to deliver an exceptional patient experience. It will be a team sport. You need the right people to help you achieve your mission. Knowing, living, and articulating your WHY will allow you to hire the right people to help you along the way (hire for culture fit, train the skills afterward), better connect with your organization (such as a hospital, clinic, or organization), or change them if they don't fit your WHY. You will be a better team member yourself and find more meaning in your daily work.

If you already (subconsciously) know and live your WHY, you will do so with even more alignment after you refine it. If you don't really know your true WHY, understanding yourself better will allow you to change your trajectory for a more harmonious and free-flowing alignment.

Your WHY comes from your past, either from pleasant experiences or deeply painful ones. The ones you want to relive or avoid at all costs.

Why I became a surgeon

I wanted to be loved and never abandoned.

When I was quite young, my parents and I lived in Kingston, a small university town in Canada. Dad (JC, short for Jean-Claude) was a doctor (not surprising, since medicine tends to run in families). He specialized in psychiatry at Queen's University. He wanted to help people with emotional pain. Mom was a sociologist, but she gave up her career temporarily to take care of me.

Unfortunately, things didn't work out as planned, and my parents divorced. At that time, divorce was not so common or accepted. My mother and I moved back to Belgium (where I was born) while my father stayed in Canada. I was about five years old at the time.

The physical separation from my father was difficult. I could see him for only two months every summer and spent the rest of the year in Brussels with my mother, who raised me on her own, while working long hours. She is one of the strongest and most resilient women I have ever known.

The time difference between the two countries and the high cost of international phone calls made communication very difficult. I felt very isolated from my father. I felt abandoned.

Of course, being a young child, I was very self-centered at the time, so I made the divorce all about me. I was probably not worthy enough to hold my family together. I was not worthy enough not to be abandoned. I deserved to be abandoned.

The pain of that divorce and separation from JC was indescribable and too much for me to bear at that age. So, I buried it deep inside. I locked it down in the vault of my subconscious mind. It took many years of personal work to bring it back up, to face the demons and work them out. Keeping the demons in the basement does not cause them to disappear. Demons are vicious creatures. They will shape your destiny if you don't address them. Demons need to be dealt with. Believe me . . . the sooner, the better.

JC was not the most expressive person on the planet. He loved me, but he was not very demonstrative. Not surprisingly, his own parents were not either. It is hard to give what you have never received.

As a result, I knew he loved me somehow, but I could not feel it.

I absolutely craved my father's love, affirmation, and respect.

Craving it meant I thought I had to earn it. I was wrong. It was always there, since I was born, but I didn't know it. I could not feel it, or experience it the way I needed to.

JC did not speak much, so when he did, I listened very carefully. One day I heard him say, "The majority is mediocrity." I am not sure what he was talking about that day. In fact, he may have said it more than once. He was probably expressing disappointment or disapproval about something random, general, or mundane. I don't really know.

But that is not how I interpreted it. I made those words important to me, like a direct message from a man whose love I craved. I made it about me. I made it personal. I interpreted it to mean that I could not be mediocre. I had to be extraordinary and stand out, to be worthy of my father's love, to not be abandoned again.

I internalized this misinterpretation of his words so much that I became an achiever—even an overachiever. I guess I could have stood out in many different ways, but since he valued hard work, commitment, and discipline, that is what I chose to do. Pick the hardest way and go for it. Go all the way, and never, never, never give up.

I was driven by this insatiable need to excel so that he would love me.

Because he was a doctor, and although he encouraged me not to follow his path, I did. I had something to prove. To him, or to myself. Perhaps both.

But I could not just be a doctor, I had to be the best doctor, in the most competitive specialty possible.

Then, because I thought that was still not enough to secure my father's love and respect, I had to super-specialize and do things that only the 0.1 percent would or could do. Who would satisfy themselves with being in the top 1 percent after all, right?

Fast forward many years later. I founded a private hand surgery center in Montreal called—guess what—"Exception MD," in a country where there is hardly any private surgery or even private insurance to pay for it.

It could hardly be more unusual.

But JC was humble, so of course I had to be, too.

So, the one person who had to be extraordinary in my practice could *not* be me. That would not be humble, would it? JC would surely not approve.

No, the term "exceptional" would apply to every patient who walked through our doors.

And I wanted to make sure that they felt exceptional. They needed to be treated as exceptional. Every single one of them. Every time. Maya Angelou said: "People will forget your name, but they will never forget how you made them feel." I did not want to be forgotten or left behind again; therefore, my focus became to make each person or patient feel extraordinary, so that they would love me and never leave me.

There you have it. This is my WHY. Raw and exposed.

That is why I do what I do and how I do it. This is why I became an expert at creating extraordinary patient experiences. It's why I wanted to go into high-end hospitality. It is also why I became a doctor.

This is where it all came from. Unresolved childhood trauma and my own personal interpretation of my father's words.

I am by no means unique. In fact, overachievers often have had to deal with painful childhoods and trauma. Enough trauma to give them the drive and fuel to achieve in order to prove themselves worthy, for example, but not too much trauma that they would have to resort to external coping mechanisms like drugs or alcohol. No amount of trauma is healthy, but here we are talking about unresolved trauma.

Magic comes from further clarifying your WHY

Don't worry too much about me now, because it's all been worked out. I am grateful for the ride so far. It is just fascinating to understand how it all came to be. It is liberating, and it gave me a great deal of empathy and caring for my fellow human beings.

But this story is also why I wrote this book. I got so much love, respect, and satisfaction from helping people feel extraordinary when they were at their most vulnerable (undergoing surgery) that I want you to have that, too. You deserve nothing less, and so do your patients.

Since that moment, I have continued to work on reframing my WHY, or my purpose if you will, from a place of healing rather than a place of pain.

Be more out of the ordinary than that.

My WHY became:

> *To treat people in a way that makes them feel great, so that from that place they are inspired to make the world a better place for everyone.*

It was a better WHY, for sure! But something was missing…

I wanted to enjoy the process, live in the present, and inspire people to work together for a common, higher purpose, what Simon Sinek calls "my just cause."

So, I revised again, and my WHY became:

> *To enjoy and cherish every moment and inspire others to feel awesome, so that together we can make the world a better place.*

What better way to do that than to create a beautiful experience for everyone you meet?

There is something truly magical and beautiful about caring for others. You, a healthcare professional who deeply wants to make a positive difference and alleviate suffering in the lives of others, are to be commended. I bow to you. You are awesome.

So, I ask again:

Why did you pick up this book?

Why do you care so much about how to elevate the experience for your patients?

Clarifying your WHY will create magic in your life. I promise. Trust me.

THE CURRENT PATIENT EXPERIENCE

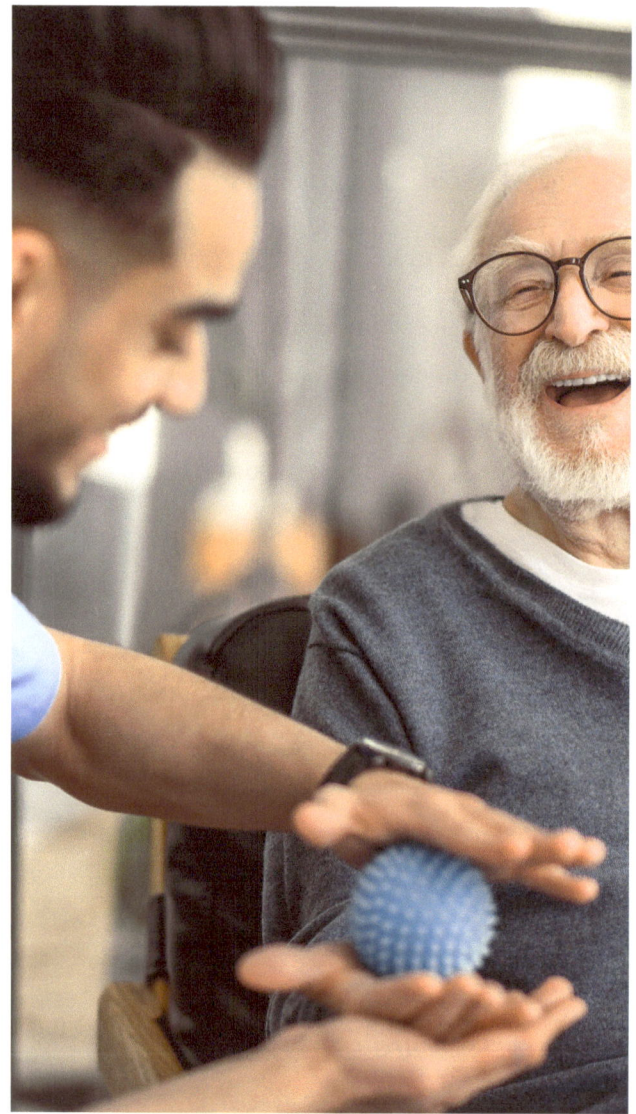
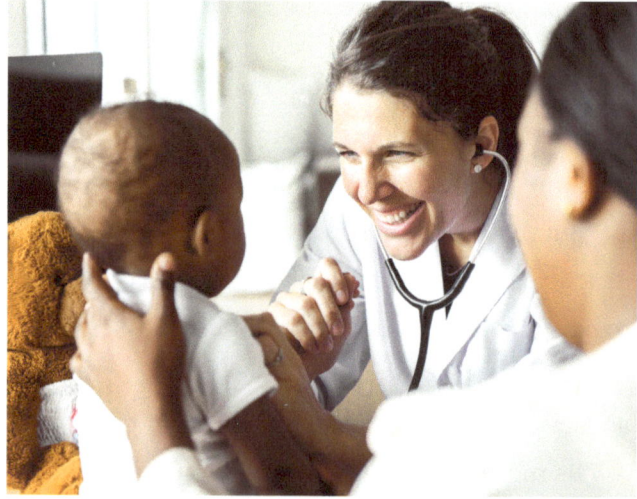
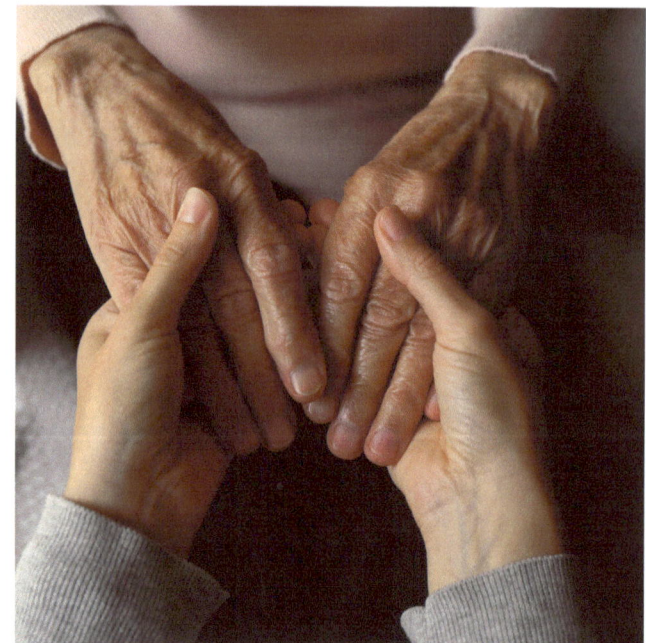

As a surgeon myself, I can really vouch for the fact that Dr. Brutus has put together a world-class structure for hand surgery with compassion, attention to details, and high technical skills in a great environment. I highly recommend seeking his care before getting operated anywhere else.

Action Step

Now that you've read about mine, what is *your* WHY? Why do you care so much about how to elevate the experience for your patients? Why did you pick up this book?

_____

_____

_____

_____

_____

_____

_____

_____

If you need help figuring it out, contact me. Email jpbrutus@drbrutus.com or find me through one of my websites.

Some great, helpful resources to read:

- *Start with Why: How Great Leaders Inspire Everyone to Act*, by Simon Sinek
- *Find Your Why: A Practical Guide to Discovering Purpose for You and Your Team*, by Simon Sinek
- The Seven Levels Deep Exercise, by Dean Graziosi, found at https://www.deangraziosi.com/wp-content/uploads/2021/03/7-Levels-Deep-Exercise.pdf

Notes

2

Who Will Benefit Most from This Book and Why

"You treat a disease, you win, you lose. You treat a person, I guarantee you, you'll win, no matter what the outcome."

—PATCH ADAMS

Who is best suited to provide an exceptional experience for their patients? Anyone who offers services where patients pay out of pocket.

An aesthetic surgeon would be a prime example. The successful plastic or cosmetic surgeon wants to have referrals coming from their patient, and they want this patient to be happy and to write positive reviews. That will impact the number of referrals and will increase their brand.

Another example is a dermatologist who specializes in aesthetic medicine, Botox, fillers, and so on. Their patient is basically a client. Likewise, physiotherapists, dentists, chiropractors, and psychologists are private healthcare entrepreneurs, so to speak. They're nontraditional businesses, typically with no third-party payer. They have a more direct patient- or client-provider interaction.

Concierge medicine, in which patients can have direct access to a private doctor usually for a monthly fee, bypassing a general practitioner whom patients wouldn't be able to see when they need them or for only ten minutes when they could. Concierge practices will often put an emphasis on preventative medicine versus ill care. Concierge medical practices take care of facilitating everything, streamlining appointment setting, and providing patients with the information they need. It's like what the rich and famous get, but anyone can have that as well. It's kind of like pampering, which, frankly, every patient should get one way or another.

If you are a practitioner represented by any of the above, know that offering an exceptional, superior patient experience is a way to differentiate yourself from your competitors.

So many benefits, too, include more money and larger margins, because people will pay for a better experience. It's called the experience economy. Likewise, you go to Starbucks versus the coffee shop where you can get a cup of Joe for half the price, because you get the Starbucks experience.

Traditional practitioners will need inner motivation

I wish every single doctor or surgeon would be interested in patient experience, but they're simply not. They're not going to make more money. There's no built-in financial incentive.

If they're caught in the system, like in the public healthcare sector here in Canada, the only way they're going to make more money is by working more and running faster. They're not going to make more money by having happier patients. In fact, it's the opposite, as they're all swamped with more patients, so they don't want any more!

So, that's not the way.

The way for doctors to embrace elevating patient experience is for them to remember why they became doctors in the first place.

That usually means focusing more on happiness.

If you're a doctor who became a doctor to help people feel better, then you become happier.

The issue with doctors is a lot of them are on the brink of burnout. If you're burnt out, you are struggling to survive and you're not able to work on patient experience. What you need is a break, and then a big change of lifestyle.

Young doctors and medical students can be pioneers

If you're a younger doctor who's not burnt out yet and you realize that there are things you don't like and notice are not as beautiful as you thought it would be, that's the time to make changes. Don't wait!

An even better time is when you're a young medical student or a young graduate, still a bit naive and a bit idealistic about what the future can hold. *You* are going to redefine how care will be delivered.

Because one thing that I've heard over and over from young medical students and doctors is that they're taught in medical school now how important it is to address the patient experience, to sit down at their bedside, to listen to them, to repeat what they say, to make sure they know you've understood, to clarify, and so on.

Except when they arrive in the real world, there's none of that. All this beautiful theory goes out the hospital windows.

It's theoretical when they're in medical school, but patient experience is practical. At medical school, training can be as dumb as giving medical students words they can learn to say to patients. Doctors aren't trained in what words to use. How do you tell somebody they have cancer? If you don't know how to say that, you're going to say it the way you've seen it done, the way you deliver bad news. The way you do it may not be the best way. But what if I told you, "Here are five different words, or phrases, or sentences that you can use to deliver bad news? Start using them, and perfect them to make them better, to make them your own."

If it is important to you, you will find a way to make an exceptional patient experience part of your experience.

Benefits for the healthcare professional

Before telling you what "patient experience" encompasses, I want to tell you what's in it for you. Today, more than ever, time is scarce for everyone. You need to know why reading this book will benefit you. You need bang for your buck.

As medical costs and insurance premiums rise, patients carry a greater financial burden and risk associated with their healthcare. Patients become more personally involved in the management of their health and in their care decisions. They focus more than ever on the return they will receive on their investment. Patients become consumers of healthcare services.

I believe that is a good thing for everyone, because everyone will need to improve and up their game for the greater benefit of everyone.

Patient demand is now the driving force. Clinical outcomes still matter, of course, as they should, but patient engagement matters as much if not even more.

Patients are looking for exceptional engagement and experiences combined with strong clinical outcomes. As they have become more digital centric and self-reliant with technology, they shop around and seek the best possible experience when they need care.

Leading institutions and practices that get this distinction will increase their profitability *not* by cutting costs (and prices) but by enhancing the patient experience and satisfaction.

There are many benefits to reap for you, your practice, and your organization if you decide to commit to elevating your patient experience from ordinary to superior, or even—why not?—exceptional. The following are a summary of those benefits.

- **Better outcomes and relationships**

    When patients have a superior, beautiful, or exceptional experience, they do better. You become a better physician as a result. Clinical outcomes improve. Patients will be more engaged with you and your practice and will be more compliant with their treatment plan. They will be less anxious and want to connect with you more (and yes, that is a good thing).

THE CURRENT PATIENT EXPERIENCE

☐ Fewer headaches

Complication rates go down when the patient experience improves.

If you focus on building a better trusting partnership with patients, they will be more inclined to follow your treatment recommendations. They will self-medicate less and communicate with you sooner if someone seems off.

Medication errors are reduced when patients receive better explanations, have the opportunity to ask questions, and better understand what medications they are taking and why.

They will also contact you before making changes to their treatment plan simply because they want to. Empowered patients enable staff to respond to concerns before problems arise.

☐ Better revenue

A better patient experience increases patient loyalty. Loyalty means that when your patients need care, they will choose you over your competitor down the street.

Too many practices and healthcare organizations take patient loyalty for granted because they confuse loyalty with necessity. They assume that if patients need their services, they will come back. Physicians still believe that great medicine will make up for poor service, that patients will forgive and forget.

They are dead wrong.

This approach may have worked in the past, but today it would be a very costly mistake to ignore patient consumerism, as the majority of patients will leave their physician because they were treated poorly by a staff member. Just read online reviews and you will see for yourself.

The patient experience delivered by the physician is as important to patient loyalty as the experience delivered by the rest of the medical team.

Medical expertise alone will no longer create patient loyalty. Today's patients want courtesy, personalization, compassion, and convenience in their healthcare experience. And you know what? So do I, as a patient.

Even in tough times, fifty percent of patients are willing to pay more for a better service experience.

In addition, it costs a practice five times more to acquire a new patient than to retain an existing one. Your patients are the clients and customers of your practice, hospital, or clinic. They should never be taken for granted, and they should feel valued, much like a guest.

With increased patient loyalty, your practice will enjoy stable and solid growth. Your marketing costs will decrease as you become better at retaining your patients rather than constantly chasing new ones. Don't make the mistake of focusing only on the value of each transaction associated with a procedure or visit. Instead, think about the lifetime value of a patient to your practice, hospital, or organization. Attrition is like taxes. It is very costly.

☐ Superior sweat equity

A lot of your sweat and tears went into building your practice. If you are running a private practice that you plan to sell when you retire, the economic value of your practice is directly affected by your patient retention rate. A superior patient experience will result in a better retirement fund for you or a better inheritance for your loved ones.

☐ Better reputation

Naturally, a superior patient experience will have a positive impact on your practice's and your own online reputation. Today, online reviews and ratings matter more than your credentials, as patients report using them to guide their decisions.

Remember, today's patient experience is directly related to tomorrow's reputation.

More than ever, patients have choices, as they should.

The good news is: You have choices, too!

☐ Better staff engagement and retention

When patients are happy, they are easier to deal with, even in emergencies or when experiencing treatment complications. Your staff plays an important role in your mission and interacts directly with your patients on your behalf.

Better staff engagement leads to better team morale and higher motivation.

Once you have a great team of like-minded employees, it becomes less difficult to keep them happy.

In times like these, when human resources are scarce, this can make a huge difference in retention and, of course, recruitment needs.

☐ Reduced risks and liability

Malpractice lawsuits affect the profitability of your practice whether you win, settle, or lose.

In addition, being sued by patients is extremely stressful for physicians and healthcare organizations.

You won't be surprised to learn that the risk of being sued increases from zero percent for those with very high patient satisfaction ratings to nineteen percent for those with very low ratings.

The goal of a malpractice lawsuit is to determine whether or not the physician was negligent. Well, physicians are found not negligent in more than ninety percent of the cases that go to trial, but

THE CURRENT PATIENT EXPERIENCE

more than $110,000 per case is spent defending those claims. That is a lot of money out the window to prove you did nothing wrong!

So, you can see that it is not only being found negligent that can be costly, but also being involved in a lawsuit. Prevention is the best medicine, and providing a superior patient experience is the best way I know how to do that.

☐ Happier life for you, too

When patients are happy, doctors and other care providers are happier. You get to live the dream. Your daily work becomes more aligned with the purpose for which you choose your profession in the first place. Less friction, less irritation, and less anger, frustration, and disappointment. Who doesn't want that?

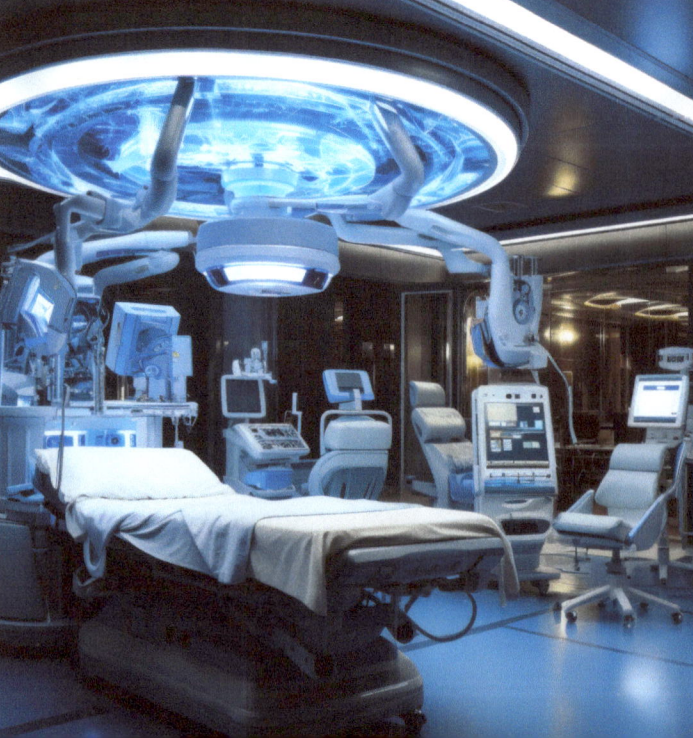

After having worked in healthcare for many years, I have never experienced anything like this. It should be the gold standard. Thank you for the amazing care. Highly recommended.

Action Step

Reflect on the benefits you get from your work. Is it money, happiness, or both? If you come up with a different answer, how would your answer correlate to money or happiness?

Notes

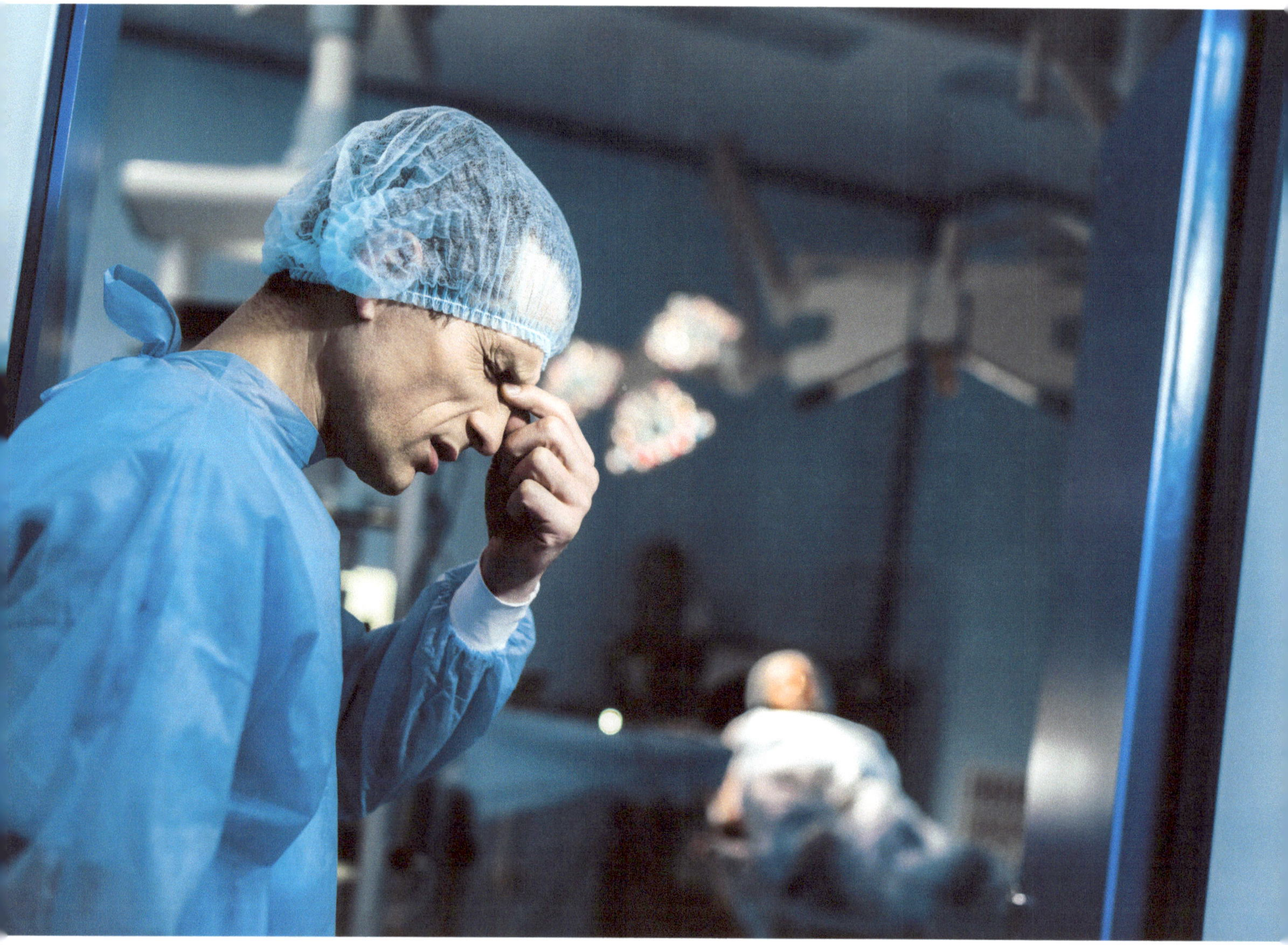

THE CURRENT PATIENT EXPERIENCE

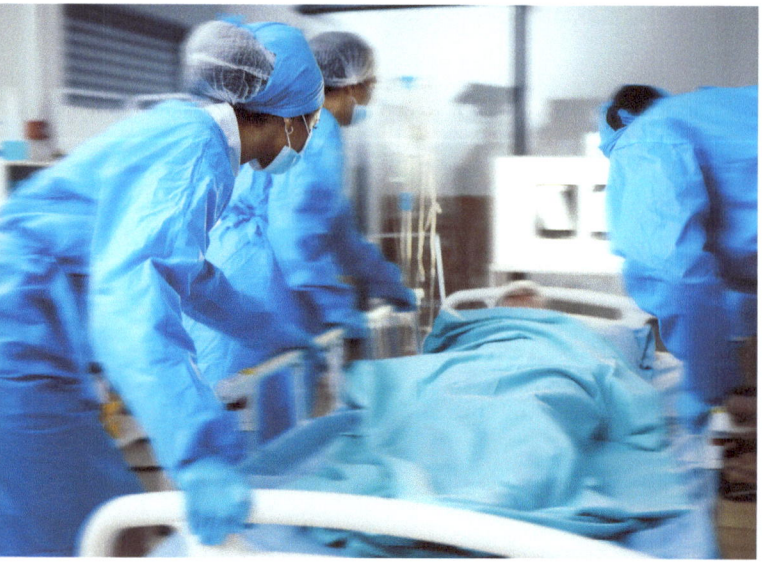

3

The Burdens of the Status Quo

"When you find yourself in a hole, stop digging."

—WILL ROGERS

At the end of the day, people only care if there's something in it for them, and the thing that's in it for them is basically happiness or money. Same is especially true for providers in healthcare. If you provide a better patient experience, you *will* make more money—or you *can* make more money if you want to. And you'll also do it in a happier way.

That's the takeaway I hope you will get from this book.

But I know it may not be easy for some of you.

Case in point: I was in Philadelphia recently for a hand surgery center symposium with mostly American doctors. Four days of presenters. I was struck by how behind they are in their inner thinking. They're still so caught up in an outdated way of thinking, which means that patient experience is not a priority for them.

It's mind-blowing.

I'm shocked, because after avoiding these conferences for years, bored out of my mind witnessing the display of ego, I came back and nothing had changed. People believe they are being scientific, but sometimes, and often, they still won't make changes that they ought to do, despite the evidence based on science.

Their choice not to adapt is made purely out of ego. (As Al Pacino's John Milton eloquently put it, as Satan in *The Devil's Advocate*: "Vanity is definitely my favorite sin." So, beware. The devil himself said he loves ego.)

Medicine is an art based on science. But as a doctor, you're not always going to change what you're doing based on what the latest study said. You know full well that five years from now, there will be another study completely demolishing the previous study. You know that studies are not always well made.

They're often flawed. Science is not perfect. It is constantly learning and revising its positions. We all know it. After all, there was a time when science said, with the means that were available then, that the earth was flat. Even if scientists all around the world now agree that Mother Earth is a globe, flat-earthers still exist to this day! So, even though you see studies coming out saying XYZ, with research literature review in place, some will still say, "well, it doesn't matter, because this is how *I* do it."

Because of such lingering attitudes, elevating patient experience really is pioneering work.

The third party promotes subpar patient experiences

In the current healthcare system, whether in the US, Europe, or Canada, patient experience simply doesn't matter. In Canada, the patient doesn't pay directly for their care. They pay for it indirectly via their income taxes. The cost of care is paid mostly by the provincial healthcare systems, as each province has its own.

As a result, because the government does not care about patient experience, as they have no direct investment in it, the experience of the patient really doesn't matter that much to doctors or hospitals either. Simply put, it's irrelevant.

It's what the doctor thinks and what the condition is to treat that matter more.

Because whether the patient has a good experience or not, the doctor gets paid the same, the hospital gets paid the same, the system gets paid the same. The inherent question defaults to:

Was medical care adequate? Yes or no?

Yes.

OK!

Yeah, but he wasn't nice to me.

Yeah, well, OK. Next!

In the US, it's the same, but substitute the provincial healthcare system with private insurance, Medicare, or Medicaid. Unless of course, you are too young, too poor, or too able to qualify for either.

For example, the doctor gets paid X amount by Blue Cross Blue Shield for caring for Elisabeth. But it doesn't matter whether Elisabeth was happy that day or not. Did she feel important? Did she feel heard? Did she feel safe? It's inconsequential.

The only circumstance where it actually matters is when Elisabeth is paying out of pocket. Because then, Elisabeth becomes a client or a customer. She's not the boss, but she becomes an important and significant character in the transaction.

The traditional healthcare systems our countries have in place have little to no wiggle room to allow for an elevated patient experience, which is why it sucks. No one ever measures or grades it. There are no metrics.

The big issue is the third-party payer. It doesn't matter to them. What matters to them is how much it will cost and, to a certain extent, whether the outcome was good. Outcome-based funding is funding based on results.

They don't yet recognize that patient experience is also a result or an outcome. But, as I said above, nobody measures it. Nobody cares about it. Just the patient.

Unless, perhaps, you're in the United States at a for-profit hospital, which is competing for patients. They are running their hospitals as a business, and they see their patients as clients who generate revenue, even though the revenue mostly comes from the insurance companies. If you have no patients, you have no income. So, there they feel a push to integrate patient experience, but the incentive comes from the business side. It's not a doctor-driven initiative.

If you're a doctor indoctrinated in this system, you may not even see the value in patient experience. You're still in this old-age thinking where you believe: "I'm the doctor. I am the one who knows," which is basically what the word *doctus* means in Latin, "I'm the important one. The patient is here to listen to what I have to say, and they're lucky that I'm even seeing them." You're simply protecting or defending your own way of doing things.

Some time ago, I was at an event organized by a surgeon who was in his seventies. He's perceived as an old, wise man because he's been around forever. He was presenting, and he talked about an unfavorable result in a patient—which happens to all of us sometimes. But he was making light of it, like that experience didn't matter.

"She hasn't sued me yet!" he said. "Maybe because of my good manners or pleasant personality!"

He was joking, and everyone laughed.

But how is that a laughing matter? How was the audience laughing about that? I don't understand. Were they psychotic? This is not something you should say.

But in that environment, everyone is so numbed to the fact that we are treating human beings. Again, I hope that the change is going to come from the young ones. The old ones? Forget it. It doesn't matter to them, and it never will.

Practitioners pay the price

The experience of medicine and healthcare has changed significantly over the past few decades, and not necessarily for the better. It has changed for patients, for physicians, and for all healthcare professionals.

Less face time, less connection, less engagement, less empathy and compassion.

THE CURRENT PATIENT EXPERIENCE

It often feels as if these essential concepts have become obsolete in favor of productivity, technology, and reliance on tests rather than quality history taking and thorough physical examination. Hippocrates must be surely turning in his grave.

Rising healthcare costs, declining reimbursements, skyrocketing overhead, workforce shortages, and an aging population requiring more care have physicians, nurses, and other healthcare professionals running to save and improve lives, often at the expense of their own.

It is hard to be compassionate and warm to patients when the healers themselves are in survival mode. If happy doctors make happy patients, unhappy doctors make not-so happy patients.

When doctors are under such pressure, they have little time to focus on what they need to do. How they *do* patient experience goes out the window, as does the reason they became doctors in the first place.

Standards of service have too often fallen below what is acceptable, with long wait times, patients not being properly listened to, unprofessional and rude behavior, all signs of a poorly managed medical practice or institution.

Any private business other than healthcare would go bankrupt (as a necessity, not a choice) if these issues were not addressed or disrupted in the same way that the taxi industry has been uberized. Even when governments and taxi unions tried to stop Uber (and its competitors) from growing, they all proved unsuccessful. Why? Because Uber listened to its customers and adapted quickly to meet unmet needs. Give the people what they want, as James Bond said in *Tomorrow Never Dies*. Inspiring words for those who wonder which direction to take healthcare.

Unfortunately, even though doctors don't always have much control over their work environment, they are the ones (in addition to patients, of course) who pay a high price.

Negative online reviews damage their hard-earned reputations, as today's patients look at reviews before booking a consultation, much like they do when choosing a hotel or a restaurant.

Research shows that the top motivations for a patient to leave a negative review about your practice are to prevent other patients from having a bad experience, to force you to be more honest about your services or policies, or because they feel they deserve an apology.

Poor patient experience and poor reviews hurt patient loyalty, your reputation, and, of course, your bottom line. Poor patient service creates a downward spiral of revenue and after-tax income. You lose referrals, and your once-loyal patients start to leave.

If you don't fix the root problem, you'll have to increase your marketing budget and efforts to attract new patients to replace all the ones you'll lose, plus the ones those disgruntled patients will talk to. A happy patient will refer one or two people they know to you, but an unhappy one will speak to many.

Just as you can't run away from a bad diet, you can't run away from bad patient service. At least not in the long run.

Spiritual toll of burnout, depression, anxiety, resignation

Beyond the obvious negative financial and professional consequences for physicians and healthcare professionals, there is also a tremendous spiritual cost they are paying.

The Western world is now facing a pandemic of physician burnout, depression, anxiety, and even not-so-silent resignation. It is not quite a silent "quiet quitting." It's more a screaming quitting.

More than sixty percent of physicians are officially emotionally exhausted to the point that they are reducing their hours or planning to leave the profession. They are either choosing early retirement or shifting to non-clinical careers. The same is true for nurses and other healers, such as dentists and veterinarians. More than ever, physicians are advising their kids not to go into medicine anymore.

One of the many reasons for this unfortunate situation is that doctors and other healthcare professionals go into the field to help others get better. They thrive on seeing the results of their actions. They fill their emotional tanks when patients walk away healed and happier, or at least healthier, than when they arrived. Human connection is what drives them. Just ask any medical student fresh out of school.

The patient experience has a direct impact on the physician experience. One drives the other, unless you are a radiologist or a coroner. A renewed focus on making people feel better can restore the sense of loss of autonomy that too many physicians experience. Focusing on what you *can* control (such as how a patient feels with you), rather than what you cannot, can bring you into a new situation from which, with a little more energy and optimism, more change becomes possible. The downward spiral can be broken.

Happy patients make happy doctors!

Are you ready to be happy again?

How COVID-19 changed patient experience

As a founder of private practice, I've been doing telemedicine for fifteen years. I've never had an issue with virtual medicine. I'm at home, my patients are at home, so we get the ball rolling. We can't do everything, but we can do a hell of a lot. And if we have to meet in person for the next step, at least we've got stuff done already, so we move ahead.

Patients want it, and patients like it. It's an experience, it's convenient, it's more accessible, it's easier, and it's less intimidating when the patient is at home. Versus: "Oh, I gotta go to the hospital where it stinks, and I have to see all these sick people in the hallways, and now I'm fucking scared."

The COVID-19 pandemic simply created a growing need and interest in private healthcare alternatives that put the patient back in the driver's seat.

There's been pushback in some countries against telemedicine, and the reasons are for all the wrong reasons: The doctors find it so nice and convenient that they don't want to go into the office at all anymore.

It's just like toothpaste; once it's squeezed out of the tube, you can't force it back in!

But we can integrate it progressively—which they should have done in the first place. Because they didn't happen, there was a huge shutdown during the pandemic followed by WTF moments of *What do we do now?* They flipped the switch and then virtual medicine was the way for everyone. Employees were then able to work from home, which was not permitted before. When the pandemic was over and employers said, "OK, now everybody come back to the office," many pushed back.

Had this been integrated progressively, employers could have said, "Twenty percent of the work can be done from home, and eighty percent has to be earned from the office, because of XYZ reasons." Then doctors and staff would have been on board with it, because twenty percent from home is better than zero percent.

As for the patients, the way they're interacting with their healthcare providers now differs from when they did before the pandemic, thanks to telemedicine. Half of millennial patients (born between 1980 and 2000) rank telehealth among their top preferred methods of care.

Patients want their healthcare experience to be as easy as their other online experiences, such as shopping, and most believe that physicians and their teams need to improve the way they interact with patients.

Digital communication is more important than ever to many patients, especially younger ones. (I define younger as anyone younger than me, and I am fifty one, as of this writing.)

Boomers (born between 1940 and 1960) and Gen Xers (born between 1960 and 1980) tend to prefer talking on the phone or in person.

Millennials and Gen Z patients (born after 2000) are more interested in communicating through mobile apps, patient portals, and online chat.

As a result of these changes, practices and healthcare organizations that use digital channels to communicate with patients have a distinct advantage over those that do not.

Patients especially enjoy booking their appointments via technology such as text and email, and receiving confirmations or rescheduling options. Things happen, and anticipating that your patient's schedule may have changed shows that you put them first.

Embracing technology is clearly the way to go, and implementing a "digital front door" is a priority. The term digital front door refers to the digital interactions that make it easy to find and select a physician or other healthcare provider, get answers to questions, *and* schedule an appointment.

Offering your patients a multi-channel communication system allows them to choose their preferred way to communicate with your practice. Remember, their preference is most likely not yours.

I want to sincerely express my gratitude to Dr. Brutus and his staff who listened, were always very supportive, and did all they could to help me when I needed it. Due to COVID-19, many private clinics had to close and the public sector was being very strict with the type of surgeries they would take, but I needed a tendon/nerve repair ASAP for my left thumb. Thanks to Dr. Brutus's virtual consultation, I was able to get it. He told me I was not alone in my situation, and he certainly kept his word.

Action Step

Reflecting on your current practice, what are three key areas for improvement based on what you have learned in this chapter?

1. _____

_____

_____

_____

2. _____

_____

_____

_____

3. _____

_____

_____

_____

Notes

4

Redefining Patient Experience

"One of the deep secrets of life is that all that is really worth doing is what we do for others."

—LEWIS CAROLL

The world of healthcare has changed tremendously in recent years, and this change has been accelerated by the COVID-19 pandemic, as I mentioned. Healthcare has been forced to go online and virtual. In many countries, traditional public healthcare systems have crumbled under overwhelming pressure, frustrating millions of patients who have been unable to access non-COVID-related care.

Expectations have also changed. A lot. Patients want convenient care, empathy, respect, compassion from their doctor and their doctor's staff, clinic, hospital, or organization. People want more options and choices, not more restrictions. Patients want to be empowered, not patronized. They want to take action, not wait for the system to do it for them—especially when the system does it in a way they don't like or accept.

Patients want to feel like they are the priority of the care system. They want "caring" put back into healthcare. After all, one way or another, the patients are the ones paying the bill, whether through their taxes, their insurance premiums, or directly out of their wallets.

They want easy, they want pleasant, and they want value for their money. The order of those things is not necessarily the same for everyone or across all industries, but the principles are the same.

How healthcare can learn from other industries

Now that healthcare is accessible online, patients inevitably become consumers, customers, and clients, and they want to be treated as such. The rules and expectations that consumers once had for digitally evolved industries like retail now apply to healthcare. Patients understand that the concept of value applies to healthcare, too. That's new!

You are now competing with Amazon and Apple.

It's true. Giant retail companies like Amazon and Walmart have entered this consumer health space, guaranteeing more disruption to come.

Take, for instance, One Medical, the primary care provider, which has about two hundred medical offices across the US. Its philosophy of care is a model designed around patients' needs, higher quality, convenience, and affordability, and they perfect this by leveraging technology. In 2022, Amazon bought One Medical for $3.9 billion to get into the healthcare space. The power of Amazon is now behind their services. The place is nice. You get to see a family doctor within twenty-four hours, or some the same day. They'll connect you with probably their own pharmacy with your medication delivered at home. Also, they're going to know everything about you, which means they're going to be able to make you offers that interest you based on all the data they have about you. And if you're traveling from New York to Houston, the One Medical in Texas will have your file. It's like home.

Amazon did the same thing with Whole Foods. They care about client experience because they understand that clients want convenience. They want easy—and they don't mind paying for it. That's why people buy Prime. Before Prime, you could get your package within a week. But the underlying want was: "No, no, no. I need it tomorrow!" And Prime was born.

You know how much money Amazon makes with Prime membership? They make $29 billion in additional revenue from Prime. It's insane.

I have Prime. I love Prime. If I need to buy something, if it's not on Amazon, I'm probably not going to buy it. Because I want it now. That's how good they are. If they have it, great, I'm buying it. If they don't have it, do you think I want to start shopping around all the different online stores? No. Amazon also has my credit card information. I don't need to enter it. Just click the Buy Now button. They're so good that, for me, shopping elsewhere online has become such a burden, compared to the convenience of shopping with Amazon, that I don't care if I pay more with Amazon. IDGAF. It's convenient. That's why they're unbeatable today.

All this to say, you don't need to be Amazon level, or Apple level, to redefine the experience for your patients. I understand you're not in retail, or in the hospitality industry, or in entertainment. But you can learn from them and apply the same principles into your world, incrementally.

When you integrate that approach into how you offer healthcare to people, of course people will pay for it. They've paid me for it for the last thirteen years—in a country where healthcare is supposed to be free. That says a lot.

Likewise, Walmart launched Walmart Health in 2019 and opened community health centers staffed with physicians, nurses practitioners, dentists, and other professionals to deliver affordable and accessible care to communities regardless of the insurance status of patients.

Do you see now where this is going and who you are going to be playing with?

The result is a patient experience economy in which not only the WHAT matters, but also the WHY and HOW.

The risk for physicians, practices, clinics, and hospitals that fail to differentiate themselves by communicating and living their WHY, WHAT, and HOW is that their services will be commoditized. To escape this destructive process of commoditization, they will be forced to elevate their offerings to the next level of economic value.

The Lanby, a private clinic in New York City, for example, clearly emphasizes patient experience. If you go there or check them out on Instagram or their website, you can see they're far from the norm. Their offices are beautiful and they offer concierge medicine, in a holistic approach.

As private healthcare services proliferate, it will become even more important to maintain a competitive edge by delivering an exceptional patient experience.

It's not a question of if, but when—and how—you will choose to enter this new patient experience economy.

Organizations understand this, and if you are in healthcare, you are in the business of caring. Caring is not a service, a good, or a commodity. It is an experience, and a very human one at that.

How a service differs from an experience

A service is a set of activities that a patient goes through when purchasing a product. In healthcare, services are typically measured by questions such as "How long did you wait to see your doctor?"

An experience occurs when you intentionally use services as the stage—with goods as the props—to engage individual customers in a way that creates a memorable event. After all, commodities are fungible, goods are tangible, services are intangible, but experiences are ... memorable.

So then, the experience is the sum of all the emotional and spiritual feelings and thoughts surrounding the service.

Emotions and feelings are what truly make the experience memorable.

Making the experience memorable will result in patients sharing your story with their friends, colleagues, families, and anyone else they care about.

Remember, whether you like it or not, there will always be an experience. It will be terrible, negative, neutral, positive, or extraordinary. And yes, you are right, it is all about *perception*. It is subjective. Experiences are personal and exist only in the mind of the individual who has been engaged on an emotional, physical, intellectual, and spiritual level. But whose perception? In this case, the patient's, of course. The beauty is that two different people cannot have the same experience! How amazing is that?

Forward-thinking physicians and other healthcare providers who are able to deliver this memorable experience will always be able to differentiate themselves and maintain a competitive advantage.

Understand your patients' perception drivers

It is natural for physicians, administrators, and clinicians to judge the quality of medical care by the quality of clinical outcomes.

But here's the rub. Patient loyalty and satisfaction are not based on the same criteria judged by physicians.

Think of an airline. Passengers expect to arrive safely at their destination. It is pretty much a prerequisite for being in the airline business, and most airlines have similar safety records. So, what makes the difference in terms of passenger loyalty? It really is the experience they get. Yes, that includes price, but it is much more than that. They will essentially judge the airline by how they were treated as a human being and as a customer. Not by the fact that the plane landed without crashing.

Satisfaction means nothing more than that basic expectations were met.

And so it is in healthcare. Patients care about how they were treated—or how much care was put into the care! Patient satisfaction surveys show that the top drivers of patient satisfaction are things like:

- How well the staff works together to care for you
- How well the nurses anticipate the patient's needs
- How much empathy and compassion the staff showed
- How well patients were kept informed of what was happening
- The friendliness of the nurses
- The amount of attention given to the patient's personal needs
- Nurses' attitude toward patient requests
- Friendliness of nurses
- Responsiveness to requests for pain management

Yes, of course, clinical outcomes (such as complication rates, survival rates, etc.) are objective. We clinicians and other professionals love what is objective because it can be measured and therefore managed.

We don't like the subjective so much because it is not scientific. And yet *that* is what matters most to patients. The patient's *perception* of reality is even more important than reality itself. It means that yes, clinical results can be excellent, but the patient can still be disappointed, upset, or angry!

Let me say it again. The patient's perception matters most! So, it should matter to you. And so should it matter to your staff.

You should all be aware of the key patient *perception drivers* that create loyalty. You and your staff should know how to create these perceptions!

This does not mean that good clinical outcomes are not important. It means they are expected. Outcomes are the product of *teamwork*. But impressions are created by *individuals*, through one-on-one interactions. Impressions are *not* about WHAT you do, but HOW (or WHY) you do it.

Here is an example. If you want a patient to know that you care about their privacy, you have to tell them. It is not just about doing the right things to protect their privacy, because they may not even notice! It is about making an impression.

How satisfaction differs from experience

Patients have pretty basic expectations when it comes to healthcare, believe it or not. They want to be treated for their illness and to be safe. That is pretty much it.

So, it is actually quite easy to meet those criteria and get satisfied patients. But the problem is twofold. One, this does *not* create patient loyalty. Two, happy patients don't even remember their doctor's name!

You would be amazed at how many patients who have been operated on by another surgeon can't even remember the name of the person who cut them open! Why is that? Because nothing memorable happened. Nothing terrible. Nothing great. Just a C-minus. No one remembers the student who got a C-minus.

What this means is that if you don't do something special for your patients, they won't remember you, so they won't come back to you or refer you.

When a patient is enthusiastic (and loyal) to a doctor, if you ask them to tell you a special story about the experience, there will always be one or more.

If you ask a satisfied patient, there will be none. A happy patient has nothing to tell.

It is the *unexpected* that creates stories worth telling (good or bad).

Non-medical businesses can create loyalty through pricing, frequent flier benefits, loyalty discounts, and sales. But in healthcare, these things don't work and can even be unethical. For us, loyalty comes from compassion, plain and simple. Remember, courtesy, professionalism, and competence are expected.

Kindness, warmth, attentiveness, and anticipation of needs, comfort, helpfulness, reassurance, selflessness, loving, and understanding—this is where the pot of gold lies at the end of the rainbow.

So, if your patient satisfaction surveys don't include specific questions about empathy, compassion, and caring, you're missing the boat.

At Exception MD, when it is time to say goodbye to a patient, I always ask:

Is there anything we could have done better for you?

This is my favorite question! Patients do not expect it. Ninety-nine percent of patients answer: *NO, it was amazing and totally exceeded my expectations!*

And that feels amazing to me and my team.

Occasionally, there is the one percent of patients who say: "Well, since you really want to know, there was this little detail that could have been done differently."

That is a gold nugget! Because the patient now knows that you really care *and* because you can do something about it. For this patient and for future patients.

And for extra brownie points, if you make changes based on what this particular person shared with you, follow up with them later and *tell them* what you changed based on their feedback.

I promise this will blow that patient's experience out of the water!

(I go into more detail about this and other questions to ask in Chapter 8.)

Forget satisfaction. If you want to play in the big leagues—and you probably do, or you wouldn't be reading this—aim to impress. Shoot for the stars, and you might end up on the moon. And that is still a moonshot, right?

How collaborating is a win for everybody

Even if those efforts aren't out of this world, you can come back to earth and go global.

Seriously. It's not as outlandish as you might think.

That's exactly what I've done with creating the Exceptional Care Network, an invite-only group of like-minded hand surgeons from around the world who are in private practice and who value innovation, patient-centric care, and patient experience.

We have a WhatsApp group, so we can communicate amongst ourselves. If we have a patient we want to refer to someone in another country, I have fifteen world-class hand surgeons who are the best of the best in the world, and I can have access to them in one minute. That's the power of the network. If I have a challenging case, I can discuss it with everyone. If I have somebody that I like to mentor, and I'd like for them to go spend a week with Dr. So-and-So in the network, I can organize it easily, and now they're going to Malaysia, benefitting from the very best of the very best.

The Exceptional Care Network was inspired by the Mayo Clinic Network. The world-famous hospital in Rochester, Minnesota, was founded by the Mayo brothers, both surgeons. God knows why they were able to attract excellent physicians and build a culture of excellence.

The Mayo Clinic created an international network of affiliated people, keeping in touch with their alumni around the world, sharing the light, and so on. On top of that, the Mayo Clinic started working with different hospitals around the world by offering partnerships. If the hospital pays the Mayo Clinic a certain amount to be a member, then the doctors of that hospital would have access to the doctors of the Mayo Clinic. Now your own hospital is affiliated with the Mayo Clinic. That is powerful. The Mayo Clinic has a brand, and now you can also benefit from that brand and contribute to it.

I see the Exceptional Care Network being a network of more than just hand surgeons, but I don't want to grow this too fast. You need to have some sort of control, to make sure the quality is maintained, to make sure the people who are in it understand that it's about giving back. It's not about serving themselves or getting bigger, because most of them have reached the point where it's about sharing and giving. They're successful already.

As of this writing, I'm planning to host our first Exceptional Care Network event, which will coincide with the annual meeting of the American Society for Surgery of the Hand, in Toronto. For the first time since its inception, we're going to get together in person, and I'm going to be able to tell them what the goal is for the Exceptional Care Network.

Most people will not go through the hassle of creating something like this. People are busy. They have their lives, their children, their career, their own thing. Few people think about something bigger than themselves, particularly doctors. Clearly what Bill Gates does is not about himself anymore. Same for Jeff Bezos and Elon Musk. I don't see an Elon Musk emerging from medicine yet.

We can talk about healthcare in the US and in Canada, but what about healthcare all over the planet? Your health needs on the other side of the world are no different from mine. It's a global problem. If you have someone who moves from Belgium to Canada, like I did, they're the same person with the same needs, no matter the location. There's no difference. Nowadays, people are moving everywhere, so it's a mistake to think that healthcare stops here. It doesn't.

It's like climate change. The US can make all the initiatives it wants, but if China or India don't do it, it's not going to make a dent. So, we need to have a more global approach to all of this.

Can we elevate patient experience around the world? Of course we can.

Just a little bit. It doesn't have to be the Ritz Carlton everywhere. That's not going to happen. But if we can make it better a little bit, then that is worthwhile.

How about the Ministry of Well-being?

While we're thinking global, let's pause and take a look, for the sake of comparison, at just a few websites for the ministries of health around the world.

Here is the mission statement from the US:

> *"The mission of the US Department of Health and Human Services (HHS) is to enhance the health and well-being of all Americans, by providing for effective health and human services and by fostering sound, sustained advances in the sciences underlying medicine, public health, and social services."*

In Canada, the federal government sets the principles for healthcare, but it is mostly administered by the provincial governments. So, let's take a look at the mission statement of the ministry of health for Quebec, where I live:

> *"The mission of the Ministry of health and social services is to maintain, improve, and restore the health and well-being of Quebecers by providing access to a range of quality and integrated health and social services, thereby contributing to the social and economic development of Quebec."*

Are you ready for some serious eye-opening now?

Let's look at the mission of South Korea's ministry of health and welfare.

> *"The vision is to build a happy society for all. This vision is supported by three missions: (1) build social and safety nets for a better tomorrow, (2) take a life-course approach to a healthy life, and (3) support stable life after retirement."*

Quite different messaging of their mission, would you agree?

And guess what? According to WorldPopulationReview.com, South Korea is cited as number one for having the best healthcare in the world in 2022!

How about Japan? Here is the mission statement of its ministry of health, labor, and welfare.

> *"For people, for life, for the future."*

Their healthcare system is ranked fifth in the world!

How about Australia? The mission statement of the department of health and aged care is:

> *"We work to deliver an affordable, quality health and aged care system and better health, aging, and sport outcomes for all Australians."*

Australia ranks number six in the world.

Canada and the USA are nowhere to be found on the top ten list.

What do you think would happen if the Ministry of Health of Quebec was named the Ministry of Well-being?

What if "well-being" was in its name, rather than the fourth (and last) of its goals? What if the primary focus was put on creating well-being for the population it is meant to serve?

What if the US government decided to switch the words "health" and "well-being" in their mission statement? What if well-being became even more important than health?

What if both Quebec and the US government introduced the word "future" in their mission statement, like South Korea, Australia, and Japan did? Would that impact their policies?

Would we then have more healthcare and less ill-care? Would both Canada and the US move up in the rankings of the best healthcare systems in the world?

I believe so.

Words have power. They convey the WHY and guide the mission.

Having clarity on your WHY can make a very serious difference. Clarity of vision and mission is power.

Action Step

Reflecting on your current practice, what are three key areas for improvement based on what you have learned in this chapter?

1. _____
   _____
   _____
   _____

2. _____
   _____
   _____
   _____

3. _____
   _____
   _____
   _____

Notes

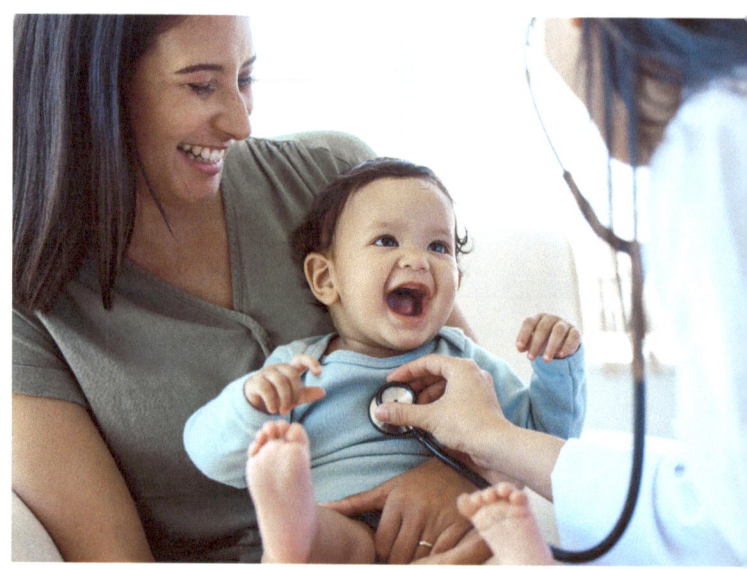

5

How Patients Will Feel in Your Presence

"It takes twenty years to build a reputation and five minutes to ruin it. If you think about that, you'll do things differently."

—WARREN BUFFET

You don't need a big structure to create change. All you need to do is do something a little differently from how you did it before. That's all.

That's going to create momentum.

It can be as simple as, when you meet a patient and discuss their issues, offering them a glass of water, a cup of tea, or a coffee. It really can be as simple as that.

It can be as simple as asking them after the examination or procedure, "How are you feeling today after all this?"

It can be as simple as putting your hand on their shoulder when you speak to them.

It can be as simple as acknowledging the person who's accompanying your patient (let's call him Stanley) instead of just ignoring them or treating them like they're part of the decor:

"Hello! Who are you?"

"Oh, my name's Ani."

"Hi, Ani. Who are you to Stanley?"

"I'm his daughter."

"Oh, fantastic. How are you feeling about what's happening with Stanley today?"

Once you start doing these small things, magic is going to start happening, because Stanley is going to respond to this. Ani is going to respond to this, too. Because wherever there's action, there's a reaction. The universe works this way. So, if you do something, something else will happen. You may not see it at first, but it will happen.

So, you can start with very small things, and those things can (and should) have an impact on you. This is important, because you will be motivated to continue if you feel an impact on yourself. That's the way it works for us humans.

Example: Interaction with a homeless person

As a practitioner, your way of being might be just as transactional and impersonal in your clinic as it is encountering the homeless:

When I came across a homeless person in Montreal—they sometimes came to the door of the car and begged for money—if I had change, I would roll down my window, give them money, and be on my way.

A few years ago, I decided to change that. When somebody asks me for money, the first thing I will say is, "What's your name?"

They don't expect that.

"I'm Fred."

"Hi, Fred! I'm JP. Here's a dollar. (Or here's whatever.) Have a good day, Fred."

You should see their faces light up.

It's not about the dollar, clearly. It's about the fact that I gave them recognition. I treated them as equals. I saw them. I inquired about them. I asked what their name was, I used their name, and then I gave them my name.

Now I'm a person. I'm no longer a rich asshole in a car. I'm JP, a nice guy.

Guess what happens when you see them again the next day?

"Hey, JP!"

They don't remember you because you gave them a dollar. They remember you because you call them by name.

If you say, "Sorry, Fred, I don't have anything with me today," they'll say, "That's OK, JP. Thanks!"

It's such a small change, and it changes how they feel. But it also changes how I feel, because I feel much better. The return on investment on my dollar is much higher. Now I'm looking for Fred, because I know where Fred hangs out. Maybe next time, I'll have a can of Coke for him, or a doughnut, or something else. Maybe he doesn't get a dollar, but I roll down my window and all I can do is say hello, and it's OK.

This will create a greater change, because the way he's going to interact with other people will be different. More importantly, it changes things for me. It makes my giving to him so much more fun.

Example: Interacting with a barista

One time when I came back from Date with Destiny—a weeklong event hosted annually by Tony Robbins—I went through a Starbucks drive-thru to get my morning coffee. I was very happy and still vibing from the event. I don't remember what I said to the person giving me the coffee. I probably asked her name and said, "Thanks, Mary. You have a nice smile. Have a beautiful day. Thank you, Mary."

You know what?

I had free coffee for six weeks!

I would go there every day, and she'd be there. She wouldn't allow me to pay for it. I'm thinking, *WTF?* I would never have thought that would happen.

That is the power of small change.

What people crave the most today is recognition. *I recognize you exist.*

That can happen in your practice as a doctor, as a nurse or nurse practitioner, as a physician assistant, or whatever your role is.

It doesn't take much, but it changes the experience.

To those of you who say, "I have no power" when it comes to elevating patient experience, remember this:

You have direct power over how someone feels with you.

That's the power you have.

Take Jeff Bezos, the founder of Amazon. I don't know him, I've never met him, I don't know much about him personally. But I do know this: If he created Amazon, he knows how to influence people to do things, because there's no way in hell he would have done it all himself. In order to influence someone to do something, that someone has to benefit emotionally from hanging out with you. Otherwise, it won't work. You could use terror, but that won't last.

How people feel when they are with you, the practitioner, *is* patient experience. With Amazon or retail, that's client experience. Basically, it is a human experience.

Action Step

Based on what you've learned in this chapter, what three ways are you presenting yourself as a caring provider of health and well-being?

1. _____

_____

_____

_____

2. _____

_____

_____

_____

3. _____

_____

_____

_____

HOW PATIENTS WILL FEEL IN YOUR PRESENCE

Notes

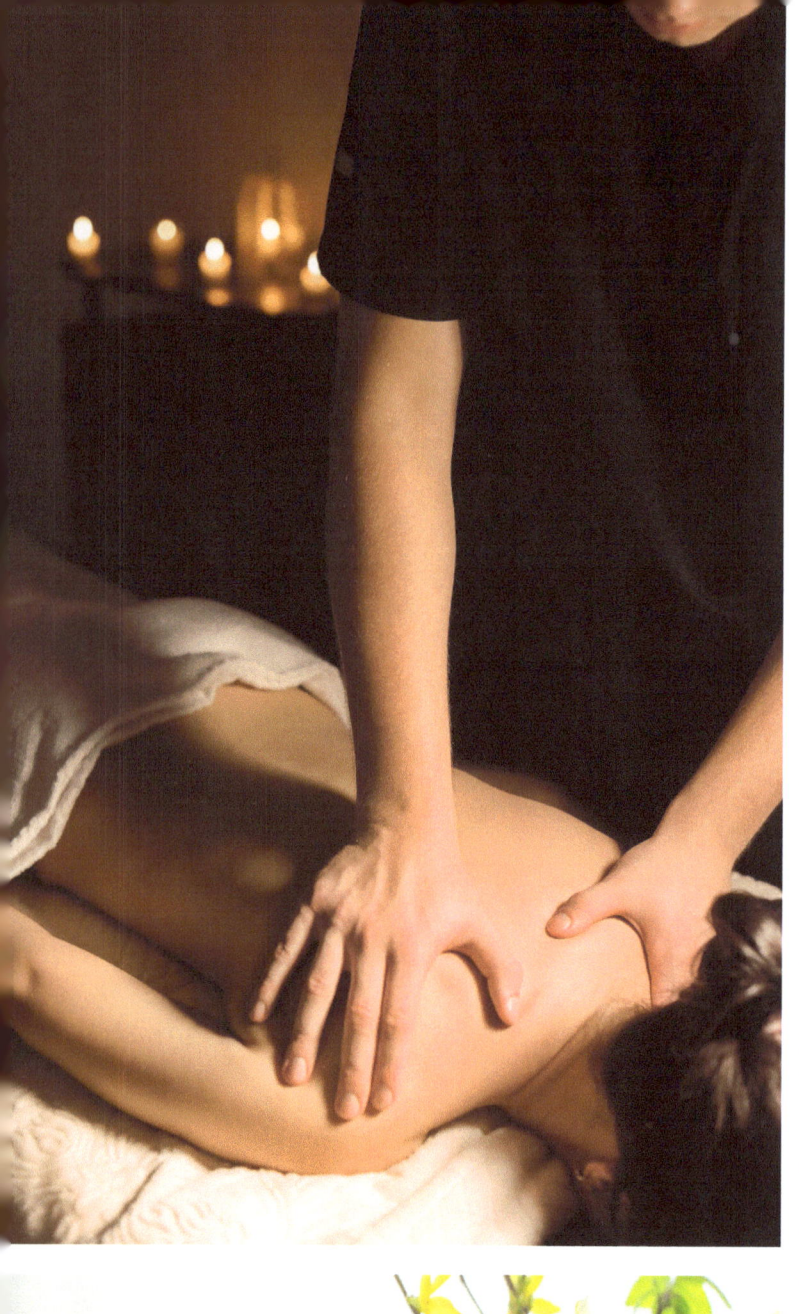

6

You're Already Providing an Experience

*"Your customer doesn't care how much you know
until they know how much you care."*

—DAMON RICHARDS

If elevating patient experience is so simple, you may be wondering, *Why am I not doing it?* Well, you might already be making these simple steps without knowing it.

You are human, last we checked, and as such you bring your own preferences into your environment. Much like making your home your own, you have the ability to set the stage for an elevated experience in your practice.

For example, many cosmetic surgeons have beautiful clinics that project cleanliness, luxury, and aesthetic taste. So, when someone walks in, they marvel, "Oh, this is nice!"

That's part of patient experience.

Maybe the employees wear uniforms. Maybe they're not wearing uniforms. It's actually a decision to have them wear uniforms or not.

It's thought out. It's designed.

Maybe there's some coconut water in the waiting room, or cucumber water to make it a little special.

That's also part of patient experience.

Maybe there's light music in the background.

Maybe there are flowers throughout your facility.

These are all pretty basic approaches you may already be doing.

Stepping it up

Scent is underused in hospitals and clinics. Usually, either it smells of nothing or of disinfectants—you know, a doctor's office smell. That's not pleasant.

But, for example, if you were to enter Exception MD, my clinic, immediately there's a pleasant scent. We have a five-star hotel lobby scent, from the same kind of diffusers used in the luxurious hotel industry. No other clinic does this because they don't think about that.

The lights are dimmed in my operating room. Nobody does that. So, why do I do that? Because it's more pleasant for the patient.

I operate under local anesthesia. It's called wide-awake surgery, so patients don't need bright lights in their face. As the surgeon, I need light where I need it, which is where I'm looking. I don't need bright lights everywhere else.

That changes the experience for both of us.

In addition to dimmed lights, we have laser shows on the walls. Patients can also select their own music, which they can change along the way.

"I want to listen to Bon Jovi," the patient says.

"OK, we'll listen to Bon Jovi," we say, and he plays.

Five minutes later, we ask the patient, "Would you like a different type of music?"

"Yeah, let's go with Coldplay."

We switch it to Coldplay, and now the patient is having a musical experience while having surgery.

All that comes from my focusing on how the patient feels, rather than my focusing on *I gotta fix this hand*. Of course, I'm still focusing on fixing the hand, but if I can't do both, a nurse or someone else can take care of the rest.

Think of it this way. Just like when Lady Gaga goes on stage to give a concert, she has a whole bunch of people who are focusing on your experience. She's just singing. She's thinking of what she needs to think of, but she's got people playing with the lights. She's got people playing with the fireworks, and she's got people on the music.

That is the reason you go to a concert, by the way. It's not to listen to Lady Gaga. You have Spotify for that. You go for the experience. How much are you willing to pay for that? You're willing to book a flight to Los Angeles, stay three days in a hotel so that you can attend the concert, which you'll pay $500 for, and then you're going to tell everybody how amazing the experience was. That is how much you're willing to pay for the experience.

So, when you introduce that into healthcare, money's not an issue. Yes, of course, don't get me wrong, money can be an issue for some people. But people will pay for what they value. Not everyone values the same experience, and that's OK.

Whichever system of healthcare you are in currently delivers a very basic experience to everyone, and it's mostly a shitty one. The only variable that patients factor into examining their experience is how nice their doctor or nurses are. *Are they nice? Are they an asshole?* That's it. But, upon reflection, they would say the rest of their experience was pretty bland.

Not every possibility is right for you

Not everyone can or should have light or laser shows or a patient-selected musical playlist.

You still have an opportunity to think outside the norm, and it should not feel like a burden. When you offer an elevated experience, it's for you as much as it is for your patients. To the degree that you can affect change in your environment, how far can you go with it?

Say you have patients who are afraid of needles, or afraid of having dental surgery, or whatever you provide. You can either drug them—America loves drugs—or give them something to escape. Solutions exist for every scenario.

Like me, you may have been approached by companies that bring you products for you to test, solutions that aim to elevate the patient's experience. Virtual reality, or VR, is one way to have them escape, and some time ago, a US company brought me a VR headset to test.

I liked it, but I prefer to communicate directly with my patients. I create an immersive experience in which I am present with them while I'm doing what I have to do. Whereas the VR headset sends the patient elsewhere.

This would be a perfect option for a doctor who doesn't really want to (or can't) engage with the patient, or for a doctor who can't change their environment. So, if you work in a hospital, you can't tell the nurse to bring down the lights. Maybe because there is no dimmer, or maybe your nurse would object to dimmed lights because they won't be able to see what they need to see. If you're in that situation, you can put the VR goggles on the patient and send them on a Mars exploration, and the experience will be much better for them. VR goggles can also be used for patient education, which also elevates the experience for them.

You may look around your clinic and see that you are already doing good things to provide an elegant experience for your patient. Or you may find that you're only strapping goggles on the patient, distracting them from noticing how your environment is not as inviting and welcoming as it could be.

But sending them virtually to Mars or another place may not necessarily have them associate *you* with an amazing experience.

If you want better outcomes, a better reputation, happier patients, and a happier life for you, then you must remember you are in the driver's seat and have the power to steer that patient's experience around to an exceptional level.

Action Step

What are three things that you already are doing to enhance your patients' experience? And how can you elevate that even further?

1. _____

_____

_____

_____

2. _____

_____

_____

_____

3. _____

_____

_____

_____

Notes

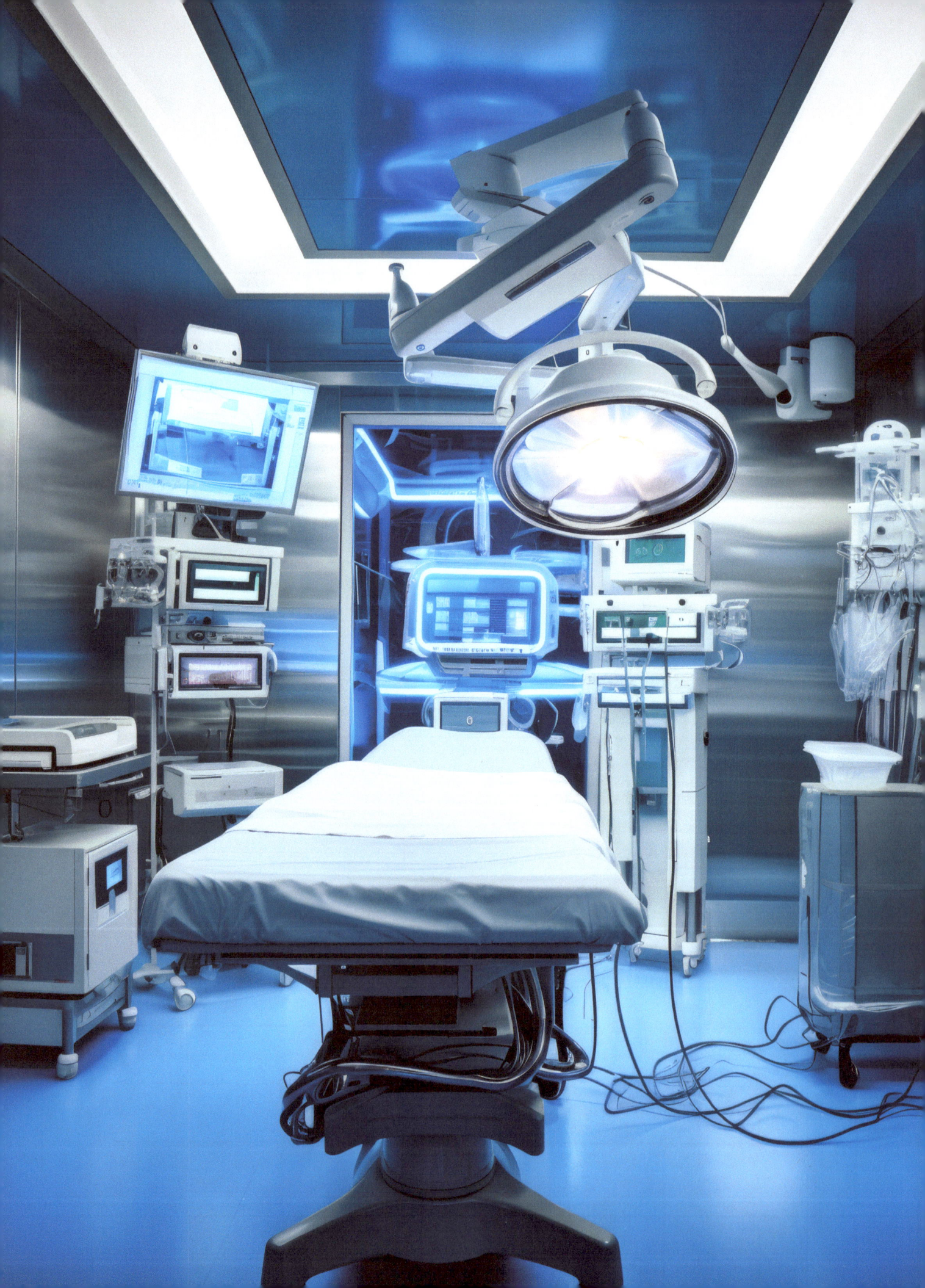

7

The Infinite Game and a Just Cause

"Asking 'What's best for me?' is finite thinking.
Asking 'What's best for us?' is infinite thinking."

—SIMON SINEK

It's important to note that there are two types of games in life that require different mindsets to play them well: finite or infinite. Finite games, such as hockey, chess, or Monopoly, have known rules, number of players, and accepted, defined goals.

First introduced in *Finite and Infinite Games: A Vision of Life as Play and Possibility* by James P. Carse, infinite games have an unknown number of participants, no fixed rules, and a moving target as the goal. There are no rules for losing or winning, nor is there a time limit. In fact, the goals are completely different. In a finite game, you play to win, but in an infinite game (like business, life, or healthcare), the purpose is to keep playing!

What kind of game is "creating an exceptional patient experience"? An infinite one, of course, one that requires an infinite mindset.

Here is how to play an infinite game exceptionally well.

Creating an exceptional patient experience is a team sport. You can't really do it alone, because every player who interacts with the patient, at every point in time, affects the experience!

The best team will be one made up of the right people, working together for the right cause. The best team will play this game with an infinite mindset, anticipating the needs of the patients and focusing on building long term meaningful relationships with them. The quality of the game improves as your experience level increases. There is no finish line.

Creating an exceptional patient experience is a "just cause" because it is truly about making people feel good. It is about helping people and making a positive impact on their lives, and, by extension, the world and even the universe.

It is a cause that is inspiring and meaningful. It is a cause that wakes you up in the morning and keeps you going. In this infinite game, the players don't stop playing. They love the game, not just the end or the win.

A just cause is an inspiring vision of the future. Our WHY comes from the past, but our just cause is our WHY projected into the future. It is so compelling that many will find it worthwhile to make short-term sacrifices to see their just cause move forward.

The concept is well described by Simon Sinek in his book *The Infinite Game*, which I highly recommend. According to Sinek, a just cause must meet five criteria:

1. It must be *for* something rather than *against* something, because it will be more inspiring as an aspiration than as a struggle.
2. It must be inclusive, attracting people with different skills and abilities around the vision of a better future. It invites the participation of everyone who wants to contribute.
3. It must be service-oriented, and those who benefit must differ from those who drive it.
4. It must be resilient, able to withstand political, technological, or societal change, or it will not last.
5. It must be idealistic, big, and bold. Almost unattainable, more of a trend or direction, like an asymptote. It needs to inspire and rally people for the long term.

As a doctor or person in healthcare, you will have victories. Small wins and big wins. But winning does not lead to fulfillment. It only gives you rushes of pleasure, joy, and self-esteem, but they cannot last.

That is why a *just cause* changes everything, because it is greater than any win.

With a *finite* mindset, you'll have days where you like and enjoy what you're doing, but you won't love it.

With an *infinite* mindset, things change. You may like some days, but you will love your mission.

It is very different from your WHY, which is like the foundation of a house. Everyone has a different WHY, but not everyone needs to have their own WHY, which is like the unbuilt house. You can join someone else's if it speaks to you, or you can have more than one.

Getting involved in improving the patient experience is a beautiful thing that benefits everyone—your patient, your team, yourself as a physician or leader, and when you inevitably become a patient yourself one day.

Action Step

What is your just cause, and how does it affect your patient experience?

Notes

PART 2

Creating Exceptional Patient Experiences

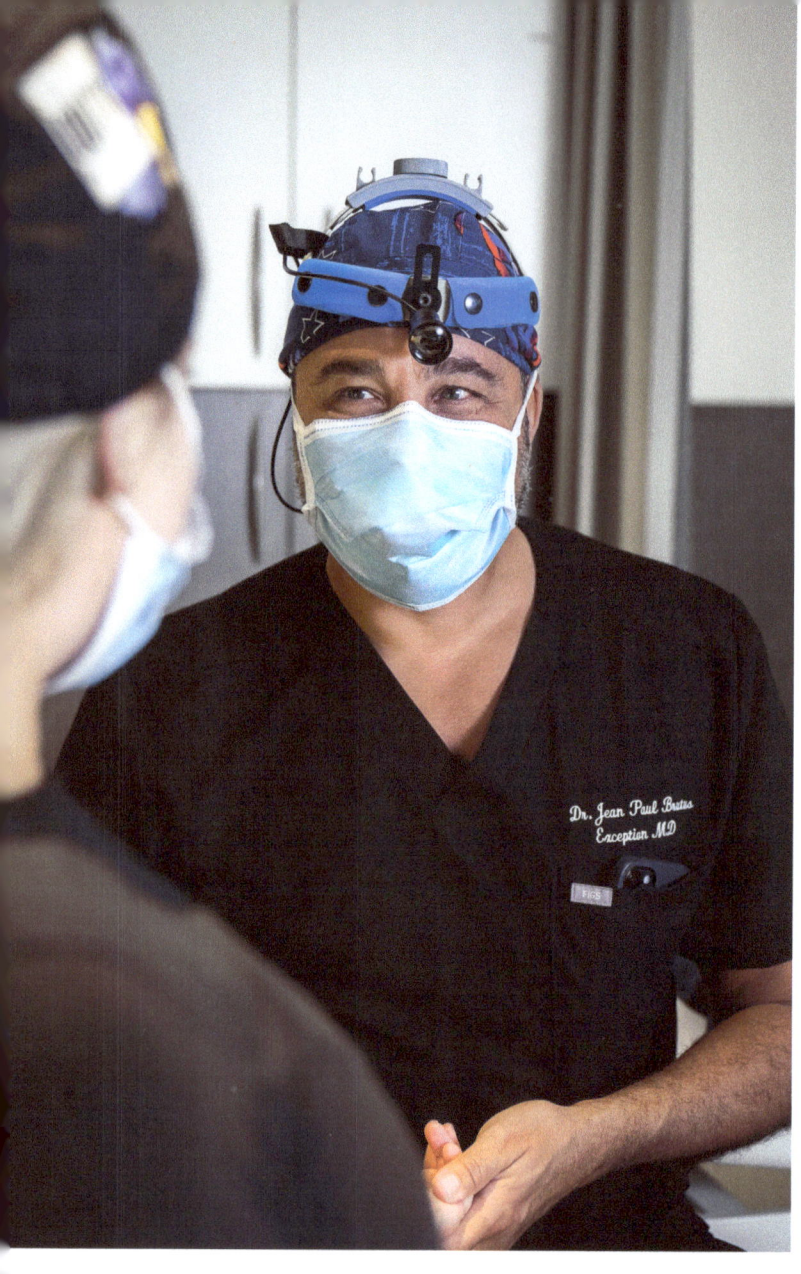
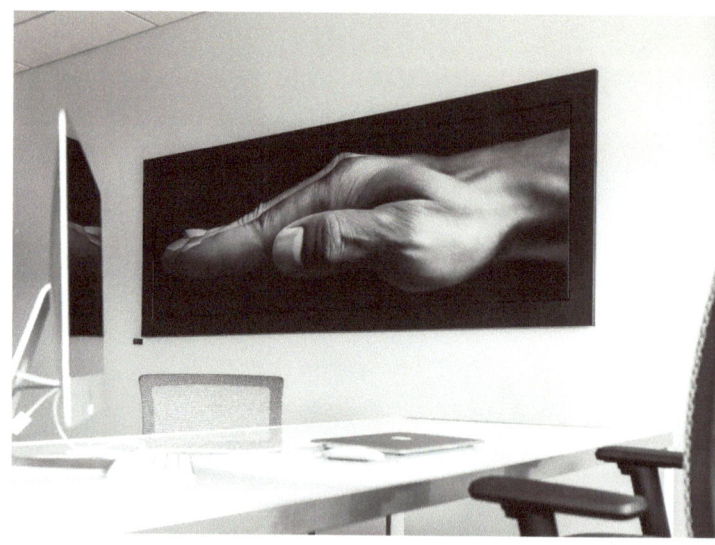

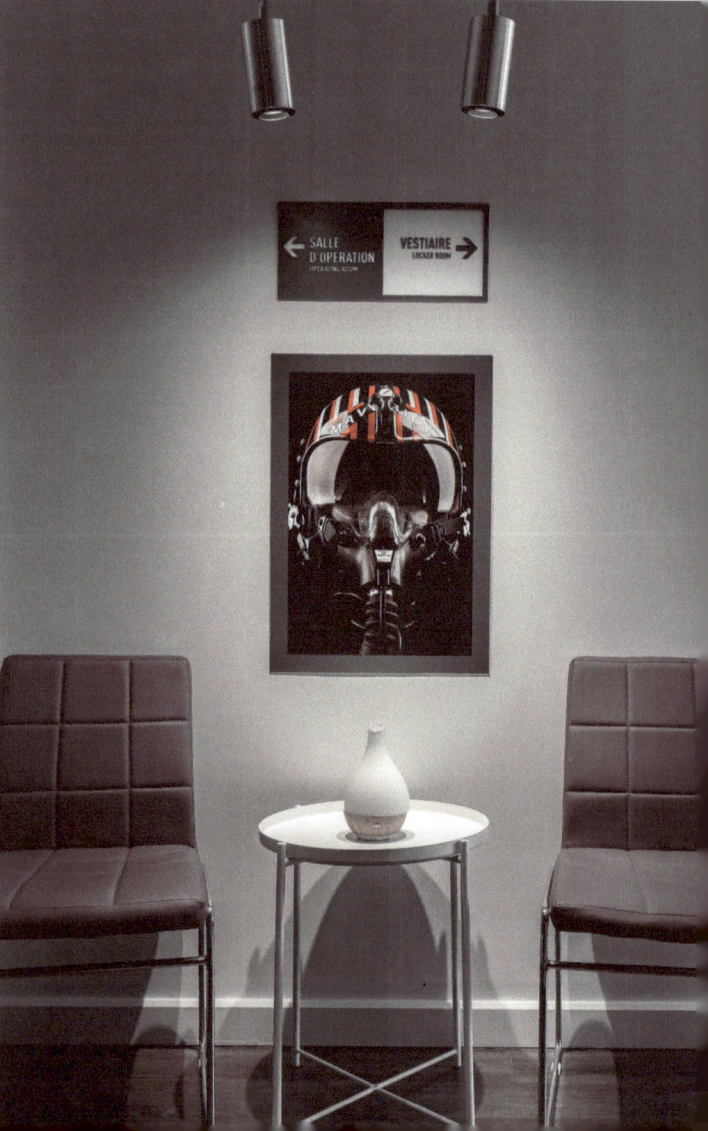

8

Start by Asking Questions

*"Measure what is measurable, and
make measurable what is not."*

—GALILEO

Can you handle the truth? It takes courage, but the truth will set you free. If you are intent on creating an exceptional patient experience, you must know where you are now, because what is not measured cannot be managed.

What level of experience do your patients consistently receive? Does your staff know what your patient satisfaction scores look like?

Leaders must do these three things to take their organization to the next level.

- See it as it is.
- Envision it better than it is and have the confidence to take your team there.
- Make it the way you envisioned it.

You will want—not need—to ask for feedback. Lots of it. From your patients, but also from their families, your staff, the mailman, the cleaning staff, the delivery people, and anyone else you can think of.

Your team has to want to be involved in getting this data, and they will be if they understand that it's not going to be used against them, but for everyone's benefit.

Know where you are. Most organizations are beginning to think of patients as customers. It is time to use technology to address immediate needs and provide a platform for effective engagement and experience strategies.

Ask your patients

There are many ways to ask your patients for feedback during and after the episode of care. You can use surveys, comment cards, or direct questions asked by you or by another staff member along the way. You can (and should) do this while the patient is receiving care, but also after they are discharged from care and back to their lives. In other words, when they don't think they need you anymore.

The important thing is to ask. But what to ask?

Here are the questions you should include because they are the most common sources of problems for your patients.

- [ ] **Was your appointment process smooth and efficient?**

    Patients don't want to have a hard time booking or getting their appointment. Use email, text, phone, or apps. Use multiple ways to make it easy for your patients to get to you. But be sure to ask how your practice is doing.

- [ ] **How happy were you with the appearance and cleanliness of the facility?**

    If the premises are clean and look well maintained, they will feel safe. The same goes for the general atmosphere (vibe) of the place. People are instinctive creatures. They will feel right or wrong in your place. Comfort will set the tone for their experience.

- [ ] **How happy are you with the wait time?**

    Medical professionals are notoriously behind schedule for many valid reasons, and some not so valid. However, if you understand the importance of the patient experience, you will realize that patients are busy people, too. Show (and tell) them that you respect their time.

- [ ] **How happy were you with the interactions you had with our team?**

    You never get a second chance to make a first impression. Every single interaction with a patient affects your patient experience, your reputation, and your performance. Not to mention your overall happiness!

- [ ] **How happy were you with the interaction with your doctor?**

    The encounter with the doctor has a ton of weight in the patient experience, as the doctor is the primary reason they came in the first place.

    A friendly, smiling, warm doctor will make the patient feel good. No question about it. If the patient feels (key word) rushed by the doctor, it is a failure.

    Remember, patients judge you on your WHY and HOW. Not just your WHAT!

START BY ASKING QUESTIONS

- [ ] **How great was the care you received?**

    For a world class patient experience, you need great patient care, obviously. That is a prerequisite. But make sure they feel they have received great care.

- [ ] **How happy were you with the billing process?**

    When patients pay for care, they deserve clarity. They need to understand why they are paying, what they are paying for, and what the value is to them. Having answers to the most common questions about billing will go a long way toward reducing friction and anxiety. Your patients are already stressed and would rather not be there. They are a different kind of consumer. The simplicity and transparency of the billing process is very important. You want to know if they see it that way!

- [ ] **Are you happy with how well your treatment plan was explained to you?**

    Each patient should feel that they have the answers to the questions they need to reduce stress and anxiety. Ask them if they have any other questions, and let them know that they can send them to you later as new questions arise. Use these questions to enhance your FAQ :)

- [ ] **Is there anything we could have done better for you?**

    I briefly mentioned this one in Chapter 4. It's one of my favorites. While not overly complex or sophisticated, this one question is the most important thing I'll say in this book.

This last question opens the door to your patient. They will know and feel that you really care about them, their experience, and their feedback.

I ask this at the end of the interaction with my patient, when it's time to say goodbye. "Is there anything we could have done better for you?" Then I stop and listen.

Nine times out of ten, if not 9.5, they tell you, "No, it was incredible," and they go on about what was incredible and how it affected them. That right there is the patient review. That's a great opportunity to say, "I'm so thrilled it went so well. Would you mind reviewing us?"

They just told you what they're going to say in the review.

Those from the 0.5 out of ten might say, "You know what? It was fantastic. It was great. But if there's one thing, it might be … when you ask us to sign the consent forms, there's a lot of signing to do. And the pen is a bit small, and my fingers are arthritic. It's hard for me to sign with a small pen."

My response would be: "Wow, this is amazing. I've never heard this. You know what? We're going to get bigger pens. Thank you for your feedback."

That's huge, because you're constantly looking for ways to improve things. You're doing it from the driver's seat, not from the passenger seat. They may tell you "nothing" most of the time, or, "listen, it was phenomenal," and you can say, "OK, awesome. Thank you. We're always looking for things to improve."

Or, they might give you more significant feedback:

"You were late three times!"

That's great feedback, and an opportunity to say, "You know what, I'm truly sorry we're late. I always make a point to be on time. But sometimes we run behind because some patients need more attention, and we don't know that ahead of time. Sometimes a patient showed up ten minutes late, and they came from far away."

They'll respond, "Oh yeah, I understand. That makes sense."

Issue solved.

But if the issue wasn't addressed, they might stay with the thought, "I wasted my time three times." That's critical, because the better you are, the more difficult it becomes. The higher you go, the higher the patient's expectations are going to become. So, if one thing is not flawless, that's all they'll see.

So, if you tell them you'll get bigger pens, when you do, let them know. They'll be floored that you acted on their suggestion, and they'll perceive you and your team with high regard.

Ask staff members

Your employees and frontline staff have critical information and insight into patient engagement and experience. Front line staff have a particularly critical impact on the patient experience.

Ask them how they perceive the current patient experience and how it can be improved. They can help you identify friction points in the patient journey, and they will recognize their own critical role in creating an exceptional patient experience.

Ask the mailman

Seriously, your mailman, your delivery people, the cleaning staff, or just anyone who comes into your home on a regular basis will notice, see, and hear things. Ask them and you will be surprised at what you can learn, even about yourself! They see and perceive things you cannot even imagine.

Ask each time

The game of elevating your patient experience really is an infinite game because you can *always* elevate it. Always, always, always.

Besides, patients keep changing. They're different. Times change. Technology changes. Everything changes.

If you don't like to be bored, patient experience will never bore you.

You won't need a shit ton of complex metrics. Just ask them questions. I promise you, they're not used to being asked. They're certainly not used to being asked by the doctor. They'll remember you asked. Because if *you* asked, that must mean it matters. And if you asked *them*, that must mean that *they* matter.

It's like when you go to a restaurant and the chef comes to your table and asks "How was your dinner tonight?" It's like, wow, the chef came! And if you say, "It was great, but you know, my steak was a little overdone," the chef may say, "Oh, I'm sorry. Let's make sure that, next time you come, I cook it myself." Now you're eager to come back!

So, just ask.

Get into the habit of asking. If you want to be representative, you've got to ask each time. Not once in a while. Ask each time. Make it a habit.

I knew that during Covid my wait for OHIP-covered carpal tunnel surgery would be so long given the backlogs for surgeries, so I did my own research online and found Dr. Brutus, who is an expert in his field and uses advanced orthoscopic techniques for the surgery. It was my lucky day! I called and went to Montreal (from Ottawa) for a consult, and my surgeries were arranged shortly after that.

Action Step

Based on what you've read in this chapter, what are three specific questions you can ask to gauge the current experience of your patients?

1. _____

_____

_____

_____

2. _____

_____

_____

_____

3. _____

_____

_____

_____

Notes

9

Principles of an Exceptional Patient Experience

"Improve the experience and everybody wins."

—DHARMESH SHAH

Experiences must meet patient needs, they must work, and they must be deliverable. Experiences are designed through a process of exploration, scripting, and staging—skills that aspiring experience providers learn to master.

The art of experience design can draw on certain design principles, outlined below, known to be effective from the practices and results of companies and industries that have already mastered the experience economy, such as Disney, The Ritz Carlton, Nike, or Starbucks, to name a few.

Design a frame for your experience

Your office will be the setting or stage for your very own patient experience.

Ask yourself what kind of experience you want your patients to have. Your physical location (and websites) should reflect that vision.

Clinics are designed to provide a peaceful and comfortable experience for patients. Likewise, modern hospitals and doctors' offices feature open architecture that allows plenty of sunlight to enter.

Often, soothing music is played, pleasant but subtle scents permeate the atmosphere, and tasteful art is displayed. Avoid the typical unpleasant hospital disinfectant smell that brings back bad memories for most patients.

Everything should be carefully designed to create a calm and comfortable environment.

Starbucks changed the typical "drink your coffee and leave quickly" coffee shop to a lounge concept where people are encouraged to linger for as long as they want, with free Wi-Fi, pleasant music, and treats. Think about it: They turned a service into an experience. And with that came a significant price increase. An increase, by the way, that guests who value the experience are more than willing to pay.

You too, as a forward-thinking healthcare provider, can make the decision to make your work environment work for the patient, not you.

So, many new clinics look much more like a spa than a traditional doctor's office. That is what Exception MD, the clinic I founded, was designed to be. A surgical spa.

What used to be called "the holding area," where patients are prepped, we now call The Lounge. We used to have quite comfortable surgical beds there, but we got rid of them. We replaced them with motorized lounging beds. They're beautiful. The patient can control the position with a remote. The lights are dimmed. There's spa music, scent diffusers. We provide patients with a face mask, thick and heavy and scented with lavender. The patient falls asleep! No medication, no drugs, no side effects. Because they're so relaxed. It decreases stress levels. Blood pressure goes down. The staff, of course, are trained to speak like they would in a spa, so we whisper, we don't slam doors. In essence, we control the environment.

Nobody else does this.

If I can do this, so can you.

Create positive impressions

Impressions are the takeaways of experiences! It is what captures the focus and attention of your patients. Make sure that positive cues support the setting you have created and are consistent with the theme.

For example, if your theme is comfort and serenity, your lobby should reflect that, with chairs and seats that are comfortable to sit in (not just good looking) and positioned in the room in a way that allows patients to relax.

Your receptionist should greet patients as they come in, or at least wave at them if they are busy with another patient. The worst thing they can do is ignore the patient at the front desk. And yet you see it all too often, perhaps even in your own office.

If the goal is to say "welcome," then everything that enters the patient's consciousness must support that goal.

Hunt and eliminate negative impressions

To create an exceptional patient experience, you need to do more than build on positive impressions. You must also relentlessly hunt down the negatives.

Remember, the easiest way to turn a service into an experience is to provide bad service! You will quickly create an unpleasant and unforgettable experience for your patient.

PRINCIPLES OF AN EXCEPTIONAL PATIENT EXPERIENCE

A negative impression is anything that detracts from the experience you are trying to create for your patient.

The receptionist taking a phone call at the front desk in the presence of other patients in the waiting room disrupts the experience you are trying to create for them.

Staff members discussing their weekend within earshot of a patient also detracts from the patient experience.

Restrooms that are not as well maintained as your general waiting area would also create a negative impression.

Keep these in mind, look for them, hunt them down, and eliminate them.

Much like weeds, they tend to proliferate if the gardener does not pay consistent attention.

The challenge to keep in mind if you want to play the game of creating an extraordinary experience is that the whiter the wall, the more obvious a little stain will be. In other words, you need to keep raising your standards as your patient experience improves! Consistency is key. Remember that inconsistent visual cues can confuse a patient and disrupt your experience.

Engage all five senses

Your life is an experience. Of the "once in a lifetime" kind. Whatever your awareness is attracted to finds its way into you through one or often more of your five senses.

- ### Touch
    One of the most important senses for human survival is touch. Not surprisingly, it is the first sense that humans develop. The ability to touch or be touched allows us to distinguish shapes and textures, cold from hot, and comfort from pain. But touch also has a social role, as humans use it to form meaningful relationships and interact. Patients also need to be touched. Respectfully, always, but touch is an essential part of the human experience. Be sure to use touch to comfort, reassure, reduce anxiety, inspire confidence, and most importantly, express empathy and compassion.

- ### Smell
    Our sense of smell is incredibly powerful. Smell is extremely important for many reasons, but also because scents have the ability to trigger long forgotten memories and take you back to the place and time you first encountered them. Smells influence our emotions, behaviors, and decisions, even when we're not aware of it. Smell is our most primitive and powerful sense. While our other senses are received first by the rational part of our brain, scents go directly to the emotional and memory centers of the brain, located in the limbic system. This is why smell is so powerful and has such a significant impact on our experiences.

Smell also plays a key role in the creation of like or dislike relationships. Smells will subconsciously influence perception and help the memory event linger. Give scented gifts and use diffusers to intermittently spray different scents throughout your venue to enhance the experience.

This is why stores, spas and hotels invest in pleasant scents to delight their customers.Smell can The typical hospital or clinic has a lot to learn in this department. If you think of a hospital right now, you probably have an unpleasant memory of the smell that just came to mind!

☐ Taste

The sense of taste allows us to perceive certain chemical compounds as pleasant or unpleasant, primarily to protect us from bad food. Taste buds distinguish five different types of tastes: sweet, salty, sour, bitter, and umami (savory, "meaty" tastes). Tastes and food experiences are often some of our strongest memories, which is why you can find fine chocolates, coffee, or candy at your favorite hotel or even at your mechanic's shop. Consider comfort foods, treats, or delicacies for your patients as a means of enhancing memory. At Exception MD, we have chocolates and candy all around the lobby, and patients love it.

☐ Sight

Sight is considered the "dominant" sense, meaning it is the sense the brain relies on most to take in essential information. Vision is essential for navigating the world, but it is also very important for creating memories. A visually pleasing environment inspires confidence and comfort. Colors, patterns, designs, and art will feel homely or professional, fun or serious, warm or cold.

☐ Noise

Think about all the unpleasant sounds your patient will hear in your medical environment and eliminate or minimize them. The sound of a staff member chatting with a colleague, other patients talking in the waiting room, telephones ringing, doors opening and closing loudly, medical equipment beeping unnecessarily, all create an impression and contribute to a poor experience for your hypervigilant patient.

Replace the noise with soothing sounds or music. Choose music that is comfortable for most of your patients. If possible, allow your patients to choose their preferred music for a more personalized experience.

All of our senses work independently, but they also work together to influence overall perception. The more senses an experience engages, the more effective and memorable it can be. When all five are engaged, the experience becomes immersive.

Master the four categories of experiences and combine them

Experiences can be categorized into four different types: entertaining, educational, aesthetic, or escapist. Let's look at each one.

☐ Entertainment

This is a passive experience designed to entertain. Unless it is interactive, you are not involved and have no control over the outcome. Think of watching a movie, listening to music, or reading a book. You can be absorbed in the experience, but you are a witness, not a participant. Bring a sense of fun to your patient's healthcare experience. Bring novelty, a sense of wonder, joy and pleasure to the care experience.

At Exception MD, before I give my patients local anesthesia, I draw a smiley face on their forearm. I show it to them and explain: "Today, my goal is for you to leave the clinic with a big smile like this on your face."

This is how I pre-frame their experience. That is, by sharing my goal with them in such an unexpected way, I surprise, relax (entertain), and reassure them at the same time. They know I really care. And guess what, it immediately puts a smile on their face, hence the term pre-framing!

Patients are also entertained in the operating room through an immersive and interactive experience with laser shows, dimmed lights, and patient-selected music. When they enter the operating room, where they are about to undergo surgery under local anesthesia without sedation (wide awake), they feel as if they are entering a concert hall. And yes, they have chosen their favorite artist.

Imagine Ed Sheeran or Elvis Presley playing for you as you walk into the operating room. Would that affect your surgical experience?

☐ Educational

In the area of learning and development, active learning experiences are more effective than passive learning. Educational experiences enhance the patient's skills and knowledge through active participation in the experience. Patients do better when they understand their health, the treatment, and the healing and recovery process.

At Exception MD, we take the time to explain to patients what will happen before it happens. We use conversations, videos, drawings, and invite patients to educate each other! Nothing is more reassuring to a patient than another patient who has walked in their shoes! They can also watch their surgery on a video screen if they wish. Many do!

☐ Aesthetics

Aesthetics is about passive immersion. You are immersed, but you personally have little to no effect on the experience, leaving the environment untouched.

Standing in front of the Great Pyramid of Egypt would be an example. You are awed by its size, but you have no impact on the experience itself.

In your office, the aesthetics of the environment should be comfortable and relaxing to make people feel good. Music, great scents, art on the walls of a beautiful office all contribute to an aesthetic experience.

Exception MD was designed not to look like a doctor's office, but more like a cross between the lobby of a five-star boutique hotel and an art gallery.

☐ Escapist

An escapist experience involves total immersion and active participation. An escapist experience takes people out of their ordinary lives to immerse them in a new place. Think virtual reality, Las Vegas casinos, Disney World, IMAX theaters, or Starbucks, where customers actively participate in the creation of their drinks by interacting with the barista.

Be inspired by the world's most successful companies in retail, hospitality, entertainment, sports, food, tourism. Identify those you most admire and appreciate and pick from their toolbox. What could you implement in your practice or organization tomorrow to improve the patient experience? How could you make it more memorable, entertaining, educational, escapist, and aesthetic?

What if you did this at every single step of the patient journey?

Do it, and with just a little imagination. (OK, not that much! Success leaves clues, so just see what works for you in other industries and adopt it). You can easily transform the experience your patients have with you, and you have with them.

Meet all six human needs

People are very different, but they have much more in common than they do in common. In particular, we all share six basic psychological needs that drive our behavior. In other words, needs that we seek to satisfy. Here they are.

☐ Security

This is the need for safety or assurance that you will survive, that you will be OK. It is also about your ability to avoid pain and gain pleasure.

☐ Uncertainty

This is the need for change, variety, surprise and the unknown. When this is lacking, you have boredom and total predictability. Fulfilling the need for uncertainty requires taking risks and trying different things.

☐ Significance

The need to feel significant is the need to feel unique, important, special, or needed.

It leads to a desire to be seen, heard, listened to, or noticed. Recognition provides a sense of validation that makes you necessary and gives you a sense of meaning and purpose.

If significance is a core need for you (as it often is in today's society), you may be driven to be successful and goal-oriented. You may have a tendency to be perfectionistic, dramatic, or very competitive.

☐ Connection/Love

Love and connection are about the feeling of closeness or union and close relationships with something (for example, tribe, family, cause) or someone. Loyalty and generosity tend to be important values when love and connection are high on the list.

☐ Growth

This is the need for expansion of capacity, ability, and understanding. It is about becoming more. People with a strong need for growth tend to always strive to become more or better. They are always looking for ways to maximize their potential.

☐ Contribution

This need is about having an important sense of service and a focus on helping, giving, and supporting others. This need makes you want to make a difference in a community. This need makes you empathetic and compassionate, and makes you want to share.

So then, many behaviors are actually ways of trying to meet these six needs. We all have the same basic needs, but the hierarchy of these needs will be different for different people.

The top two of your needs are the most predictive of your behavior and are called personality drivers.

Knowing which two of your six human needs are your primary drivers affects your ability to connect with others and develop healthy relationships, and is essential to understanding what stimulates and motivates you.

It will also help you understand and eliminate your triggers so that you can be in control of your emotions instead of your emotions being in control of you.

Understanding and mastering the psychology of the six human needs described by Chloe Madanes will be important for you as the leader of your patient experience.

If you know your patients well, or learn to read their needs well, you will be able to provide them with a much more personalized and superior experience. This is one of the fundamentals of creating a truly exceptional patient experience.

And yes, you guessed it. It applies not just to patients, but to all the people you meet in life and want to give an experience to. Life is nothing but an experience, isn't it?

Now, you may be thinking that you don't have enough time to analyze the psyche of each of your patients, and that's fair (although it really doesn't take much time). As with anything else, remember that practice makes perfect…

But if you don't have the time or desire to become a very practical psychologist to improve your patient experience, just make sure all six needs are met throughout the patient journey.

Make your patients feel loved and connected to you, your staff, and your other patients (sense of community).

Make them feel safe with you, your environment, and your team. Let them know they are truly cared for. Sure, tell them, why not?

Create surprises of the pleasant kind in their journey (gifts, personalized unexpected attention, a written birthday card or note, a well-wishing card…).

Educate, educate and educate your patients and their significant family members (they are usually with them, right?) so that they learn and feed the need to grow throughout their experience with you.

Allow them to share the benefits of their growth with others by becoming advocates, mentoring patients, or contributing to a philanthropic cause you support. Encourage them to reassure or comfort other patients who are going through a similar journey. Be creative in how you meet their need to share.

Make your patients feel that they are important to you as a person and that you care about getting to know them. Let them know that you value their trust, recognize their uniqueness, and ensure that their need for meaning is met.

Identifying and meeting a patient's two driver needs is a sure way to quickly connect with them on a deeper level. Satisfying all six of these basic needs throughout the patient journey is the way to create a magical experience.

Offer your patient a memory to take home

Certain goods are purchased primarily for the memories they convey.

Vacationers buy postcards, golfers buy T-shirts or caps to commemorate a course, concertgoers take home T-shirts. Fancy restaurants run by celebrity chefs sell recipe books—these memorabilia are physical reminders of an experience.

PRINCIPLES OF AN EXCEPTIONAL PATIENT EXPERIENCE

At Exception MD, patients are given a heartwarming character named Exceptional Eugene. He (not it) is a character at Exception MD. He comes in the form of a stress ball with goofy eyes and an awkward smile, but he is truly a person, a companion, a patient buddy. Patients meet Eugene on the day of surgery while waiting in the surgical holding area, aka The Lounge, before receiving local anesthesia. Eugene is literally placed in the patient's hand so they can focus on him and play with him while they wait. It gives them something to do and a sense of control. They ask questions about Eugene's role and name (Eugene pleasantly surprises them) and are playfully told that he will be the captain of their rehabilitation team after surgery. He will accompany the patient in the operating room as a comfort buddy. (Remember the little teddy bear you used to carry around with you as a child to feel safe?)

Because we personalized Eugene by making him a character (remember Disney?), patients develop a relationship with him. They take Eugene on vacation and send us pictures of Eugene on vacation with them. We post these pictures of Eugene traveling around the world on social media. That is the power of character creation!

Exception MD is all about making everyone feel like an exception to the rule. Everyone is a super VIP.

We use the slogan "I am an exception" or "Je suis une exception" as a constant reminder of how unique each of our patients is. We have it framed on the wall and printed on stylish and comfortable hoodies. Patients love to buy these hoodies because they look cool and they remind them of their experience! Our goal is not to make money with merchandise, but to make memories!

Starbucks, Mindgeeks, Disney, Sandals, Club Med, Ritz Carlton are examples of companies that give their customers such an amazing experience that they actually want to take home memories.

Ask yourself this question:

Would one of your patients buy something from you to remember their experience with you?

If not, what could you do to change that?

Surgery was a breeze. It felt like a spa. I was offered coffee and a homemade cupcake after surgery. Follow-up was done remotely almost every day.

I have never before experienced this. Our hospitals have much to learn. Thank you to the whole team. You made a world of difference in my life. Hands are 100%!

PRINCIPLES OF AN EXCEPTIONAL PATIENT EXPERIENCE

Action Step

What are three practical changes or adjustments you can make in your daily interactions with patients to improve their experience, given the principles discussed in this chapter?

1. _____

_____

_____

_____

2. _____

_____

_____

_____

3. _____

_____

_____

_____

Notes

10

Create an Exceptional Patient Experience Program

"A customer is the most important visitor on our premises. He is not dependent on us. We are dependent on him. He is not an interruption in our work. He is the purpose of it. He is not an outsider in our business. He is part of it. We are not doing him a favor by serving him. He is doing us a favor by giving us an opportunity to do so."

—MAHATMA GANDHI

Do you want to really completely transform your patients' experience? If so, then you can create and design a patient experience program.

Questions to ask yourself: How are you going to do this? Who's going to be leading the experience and the program? How are you going to make sure the program works? Are you going to measure the effects of your changes?

Designing a patient experience program is an organized way of enhancing patient experience, and it's a rewarding team effort. It's systemized versus being too complex. For me, all I like to do is a few tweaks here and there. I ask myself constantly, what are the things that I can do?

You can read through this chapter and pick only a handful of things to do, and that's it. In that case, you won't need a whole system for this because you just want to make the experience you provide slightly better; you're not seeking a complete transformation or to blow them out of the water. It depends on what your goal is.

I would be very surprised if anyone wanted a complete makeover because their patient experience was so bad. What they're going to want is to make it a little bit better, then a little bit better, and then a little bit better. I don't think you'd want to go from one extreme to the other.

Not everybody wants to be the Ritz Carlton, and not everybody can. Clearly, Walmart may be interested in improving their client/patient experience, but they're not going to do it the same way as the Ritz Carlton would. They don't have the same margins, they don't have the same clientele, and their patients or clients don't want the same things.

It's still interesting, for those who want to elevate their experience, to understand how the masters do it. Because the masters—Disney, Ritz Carlton, Starbucks, and all the giants—have a recipe.

It's not magic. They call it the Magic Kingdom, but it's not magic. Magic is tricks that are so well executed that you don't see them, and sometimes, even as you're looking at them—you know they're tricks—and you still can't see them. That's the kind of magic you can convey when you employ these steps and elevate your patient experience.

The goal here is to provide practical ways to do this, in accordance with what it is that you want to do. It's not everyone's cup of tea, but I hope it's yours because you picked up this book. It will take dedication, an open mind, and a desire for change. It will increase patient loyalty, but most importantly, it will bring more meaning and joy to patients and caregivers.

If you are ready, here are seven steps to creating an exceptional patient experience program.

Step 1: Assess the current state of affairs

You already have a brand and your patients have an experience, so before you invest efforts to change it, you need to know what it is.

There are several ways to gather patient feedback.

You can give patients a patient satisfaction survey and get anonymous feedback to help you understand where you stand.

Use existing surveys or create your own based on your practice's needs. Consider giving the survey to the patient at checkout, mailing the survey, or sending it via email.

Limit the number of surveys or set a time period for the survey to avoid survey fatigue. Distribute the survey to all patients or ensure that patients are randomly selected to receive the survey.

You can also mail or email the survey, along with a brief cover letter introducing the survey and its importance to improving the patient experience in your practice. This will increase your response rate.

Your survey should be short and simple, asking about ease of access, patient perception of teamwork, ease and friendliness of communication, front desk hospitality, office cleanliness, and billing transparency.

You can also ask members of your team to have casual conversations with patients during their clinic visit and get a pulse on the patient experience by simply asking them such questions as "How was your visit today?" and "Do you have any feedback you'd like to share?" These questions can be asked by a receptionist at checkout, or by a medical assistant when escorting the patient out of the exam room at the end of the visit. Any pertinent feedback, positive or negative, should be relayed to the practice manager.

Reviewing patient complaints (and online comments or complaints) will also provide perspective on what is not going as well as it could.

Reviewing the data will allow you to identify themes and trends and provide direction for the desired guiding principles of your program.

Step 2: Define your objective

You will need to decide what your practice will strive for and what will guide the purpose and structure of your program. Involving your team members is important at this stage because improving the patient experience is a team sport. Understanding their perspectives will be critical to success. Have your team define the ideal patient experience and outline the goals of the program. Your goal can be defined by your mission statement.

For example, "Patients First" at the Cleveland Clinic.

Step 3: Engage other physicians, staff, and other team members

Improving the patient experience is a team sport, and improving the culture is essential to creating a sustainable patient experience program.

To be successful as the leader of this initiative, you must involve the entire clinical care team, administrative, front desk and scheduling staff, physicians, and, most importantly, your patients in the creation of this program.

Discuss the results of your assessment of your practice's current patient experience and brainstorm initiatives for your patient experience platform. Use these discussions to identify areas where training would be useful.

Step 4: Develop and implement your patient experience strategy

Decide with your team which changes to implement first. Starting small is critical to making changes sustainable and scalable. Slow and steady wins the race, every time.

Encourage feedback and constructive criticism to improve the practice, achieve your goals, and provide better care to patients. Engage with patients to gain understanding of tactics to strengthen both the practice and the perception of care.

Without employee engagement, there is little chance of success. Actively listening to your employees with empathy is critical, but it is not enough. Make positive changes to the work environment based on the input you receive from your team of employees. When employees feel listened to, they become more engaged. More engaged employees make for happier patients.

Service excellence training is important, but it will not prevent all service failures. By developing a strong service recovery strategy, you can turn a frustrated patient into a raving fan of your practice. While all staff should be prepared to handle these types of situations, it is probably a good idea to designate one person to lead service recovery efforts. Look for opportunities to provide immediate service recovery and feedback to staff and physicians. Train for these valuable opportunities. When you solve a problem, think of it as solving two problems. The one you have in front of you now, and the same one you will deal with in the future by preventing it based on what you have learned now.

Step 5: Teach effective and empathic communication

Strong relationships with patients are built on effective communication. Practice empathic listening to improve your own communication skills.

Listening with empathy is about understanding your patient's experience. It is the ability to put yourself in their shoes, to feel what they are going through, and to share their emotions.

It is recognizing and validating (not dismissing or minimizing) a patient's fear, anxiety, pain, and worry and understanding the patient's feelings to facilitate better care.

Step 6: Get feedback and adjust

If your initiatives are aimed at solving a specific problem, get feedback on the patient experience around that specific issue.

For example, patients may have been particularly dissatisfied with wait times in your office (a common challenge for physicians), so you implemented a process for the care team to notify the front desk when the physician is running behind schedule.

As a result of the new initiative, patients can be notified before they arrive or when they check in. They can even be offered the opportunity to reschedule if they prefer. You can assess the impact of this initiative on the patient experience by surveying patients on this specific aspect.

You can also get valuable feedback from the front desk team. In addition, by sharing what you learn, you will foster an environment of continuous quality improvement to keep employees engaged. You can share this feedback in meetings or via email, daily huddles, or even displays, such as a visual management board in the break room or cafeteria.

Step 7: Celebrate and recognize accomplishments. Keep going!

Building a patient experience program can be challenging because it requires a shift in healthcare thinking. Keep your team on board by demonstrating value. Continue to solicit employee feedback and suggestions for improving the program. Make a habit of sharing survey results and feedback. More importantly, share patient stories. Celebrate the team members who shine in your initiative.

I had a very hard time finding a doctor that was able to take on my case and/or help me. I saw a surgeon prior to Dr. Brutus, and he was a nightmare. The first time I walked into Dr. Brutus's office, I was extremely relieved. I had been in pain from my injury for a year and a half, and no one could help. I felt hopeless. He took the time to listen to me and answered all my questions. When we ran out of treatments and decided that surgery was the next step, he took the time to explain the procedure and the healing process to me. We had constant follow-up appointments every six to eight weeks following occupational therapy, so he could make sure I was healing properly. He also convinced me to quit smoking prior to my surgery. He is an EXCEPTIONAL doctor. His staff is great as well, always smiling and so polite. He is always punctual. Thank you, Dr. Brutus, for everything you have done for me. Keep doing what you're doing because clearly you've got it right!

Action Step

Given the content covered in this chapter, what are three strategies or tools you can implement to actively engage patients in their care and empower them to make informed decisions?

1. _____

_____

_____

_____

2. _____

_____

_____

_____

3. _____

_____

_____

_____

Notes

CREATE AN EXCEPTIONAL PATIENT EXPERIENCE PROGRAM

I am a professional pianist/composer and last October was diagnosed with what is called extensor tendon sagittal band rupture and instability. This condition threatened to end my career; however, I was most fortunate to have had Dr. Brutus recommended to me. After some consultation and a feeling of confidence in what could be, I decided to have Dr. Brutus proceed with surgical repair and stabilization of the extensor tendons. The surgery was more than successful. It was followed by therapy by a wonderful therapist recommended by Dr. Brutus, and approximately five months later, I was able to return to my work as if nothing had ever transpired. I will ever be indebted to Dr. Brutus for his special skills and professionalism. He is one of a kind.

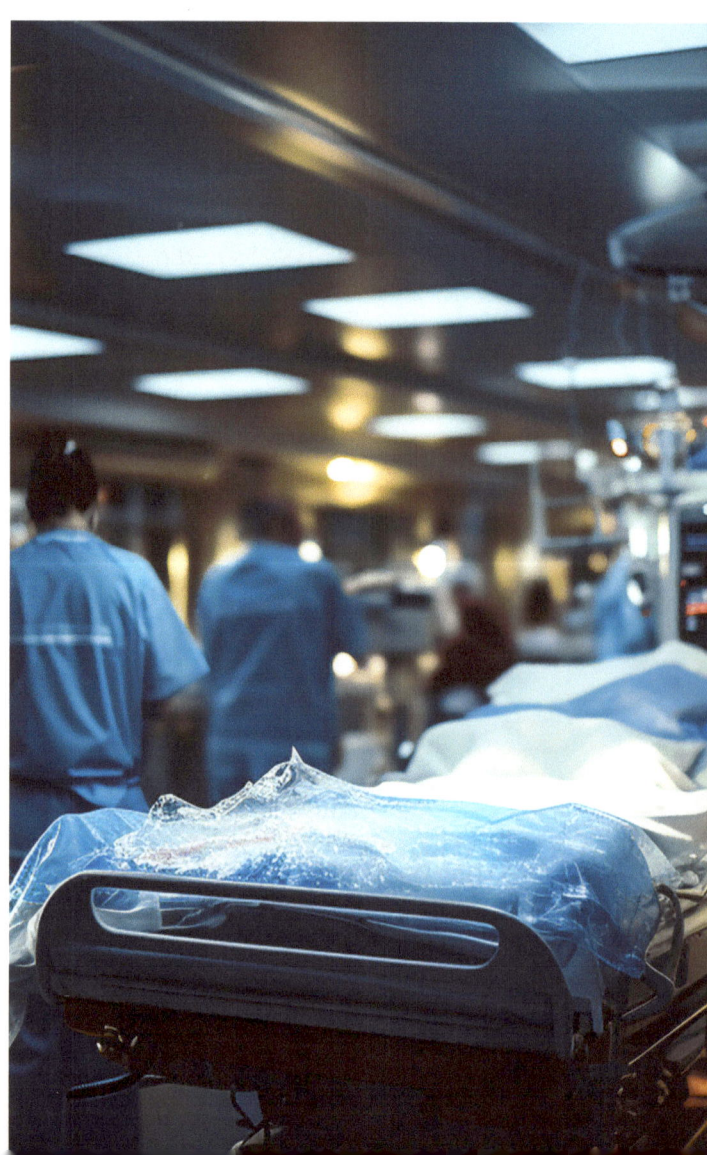

11

Understand Your Patient's Journey

"Your most unhappy customers are your greatest source of learning."

—BILL GATES

Understanding the patient journey is critical to delivering an exceptional patient experience. The patient journey refers to the series of interactions and experiences a patient goes through from the first point of contact with a healthcare practice to the final post-treatment follow-up. Understanding the patient journey allows healthcare entrepreneurs to identify pain points and opportunities to improve the patient experience.

Map the patient journey

To understand the patient journey, it is helpful to map it. This can be done by walking through the process from the patient's perspective, identifying each step and touchpoint along the way. Some key touchpoints to consider are:

- First point of contact (e.g., phone call, website visit)
- Scheduling an appointment
- Arriving at the practice
- Check-in and registration
- Consultation with a healthcare professional
- Diagnosis and treatment planning
- Treatment and follow-up
- Billing and payment

It is also important to consider the patient's emotional state at each touchpoint. For example, a patient may be anxious or stressed about scheduling an appointment, but feel relieved after a successful consultation.

Gather patient feedback

Once the patient journey has been mapped, it is important to gather feedback from patients to understand their experience. This can be done through surveys, interviews, and focus groups. It is important to gather feedback from patients at different touch points along the journey to get a complete picture of their experience.

Analyze the patient journey

Once feedback is collected, it is important to analyze it to identify pain points and opportunities for improvement. This can be done by looking for patterns and themes in the feedback. For example, if several patients report long wait times, this may indicate an opportunity to improve the scheduling process.

Implement changes

Once pain points and opportunities for improvement have been identified, it is important to implement changes to improve the patient experience. This may involve making changes to processes, training staff, or incorporating new technology. It is important to involve patients in the change process to ensure that their feedback is considered and that changes are aligned with their needs and preferences.

Their whole staff is incredibly helpful and caring. Went through a triple procedure and recovered within a week. They helped me get over my PTSD and were always there to answer and reassure my doubts. Thanks again for everything.

Action Step

After mapping your patient journey, what opportunities for improvement have you identified that could include the patient experience?

_____

_____

_____

_____

_____

_____

_____

_____

_____

_____

_____

_____

Notes

12

Identify Your Ideal Patient's Needs and Preferences

"The more you engage with customers the clearer things become and the easier it is to determine what you should be doing."

—JOHN RUSSELL

Understanding the needs and preferences of your ideal patients is critical to business success. By identifying these needs and preferences, healthcare entrepreneurs can tailor their services and marketing efforts to attract and retain their ideal patient population. This can lead to increased revenue and profitability, as well as improved patient outcomes.

Define your ideal patient

The first step in identifying your ideal patient is to define who they are. This can be done by considering factors such as demographics, medical conditions, and insurance coverage. It may also include consideration of factors such as lifestyle, values, and personality.

By defining your ideal patient, you can better understand their needs and preferences and tailor your services and marketing efforts to attract and retain them. You cannot be everything to all patients, but you can be to your ideal patients by truly catering to their needs.

Gather patient information

Once you have defined your ideal patient, it is important to gather information about them. This can be done through patient surveys, interviews, and focus groups. It can also be gathered through electronic health records, which can provide information about a patient's medical history, medications, and allergies.

It's also important to pay attention to patient feedback, as it can provide valuable insight into their needs and preferences.

Seeking to understand the psychology and motivations of your ideal patients will be a very smart decision, as it will support your mission to fulfill their needs.

Create patient personas

Creating patient personas can be a helpful tool to better understand your ideal patients. Patient personas are fictional representations of your ideal patients based on the information you have gathered. They can include information such as demographics, medical history, and communication preferences.

By creating patient personas, you can better understand the unique needs and preferences of your ideal patients and improve the ways you interact with them.

Analyze patient data

It is also important to analyze the patient data you have collected to identify trends and patterns that align with your ideal patient population.

By identifying these trends and patterns, you can better understand the needs and preferences of your ideal patient population and tailor your services, communication, and marketing efforts accordingly.

Implement changes

Once you have identified the needs and preferences of your ideal paticnt population, it is important to implement changes to attract and retain them. This may involve changes to your facility, services, and continued staff training. It may also involve incorporating new technologies, such as telemedicine, to better meet the needs of your ideal patients. It may also involve implementing targeted marketing and messaging strategies that appeal to your ideal patient population.

. . . Surgery day was smooth and even enjoyable. They had music and a lightshow in the operating room. Local anesthesia. Zero pain.

I even got to choose the color of my dressing!

I walked out of the operating room, like it was nothing.

After surgery, I had phone calls almost every day to check on me.

Customer service above any expectations from scheduling my first appointment to my follow-up. Would definitely recommend it to anyone looking for care in this field. Five-star experience.

Action Step

What are the key qualities of your ideal patient?

Notes

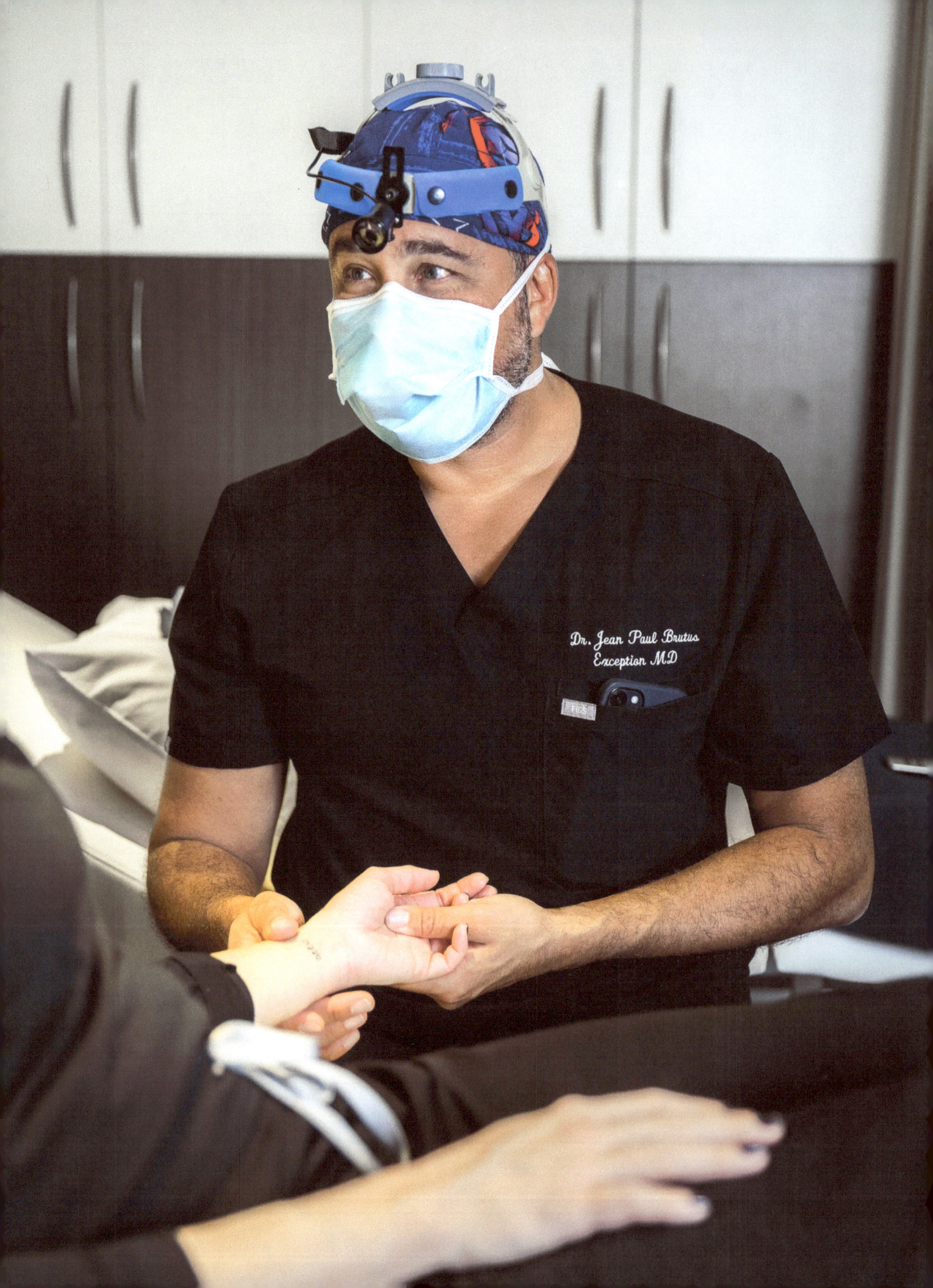

13

Optimize Onboarding of Your Ideal Patient

"It is not the strongest of the species that survives, nor the most intelligent, but the one most responsive to change."

—CHARLES DARWIN

When it comes to attracting new patients, it is not only important to optimize the initial contact, but also to focus on attracting the right patients—those who are the best fit for your practice. Don't scream from the top of the mountain with the biggest bullhorn. Aim to whisper to the ones you want to serve. By identifying and targeting your ideal prospects, you can increase the chances of converting them into actual patients and improve the overall patient experience.

Today's patients expect a high level of communication and convenience from healthcare providers. They want to be able to easily access information and communicate with their healthcare provider through multiple channels such as phone, email, and online portals.

Social media

Regularly monitor social media accounts and respond promptly to inquiries, comments, and messages by potential patients. This shows them your practice values their time and is committed to providing exceptional service.

Have a script or policy for responding to social media inquiries that includes important information such as the practice's services, hours of operation, and location.

On your social media accounts, make it clear what your practice's contact information, services offered, and hours of operation are so that new patients can easily contact your practice when they need to.

When responding to their messages, use a professional and friendly tone, similar to how high-end hotels provide personalized and friendly service to their guests.

Be transparent and provide accurate information on social media to build trust with potential patients.

Make sure you're responsive and timely in responding to messages. By optimizing responses to potential new private patients via social media, you can create a positive first impression and increase the likelihood of converting prospective patients into actual ones.

Always keep in mind that confidentiality is of the utmost importance in our profession, so redirect to other more secure means of communication when patients ask you specific questions.

Remember, you do not own Instagram or Facebook Messenger. Those communications are not private.

Email communication

Optimize and personalize responses to initial emails from potential patients. Create personalized email templates that can be quickly and easily customized for each potential patient. These templates should include a warm professional greeting, information about the practice's services and availability, and a clear call to action, such as scheduling an appointment or requesting more information.

To personalize the email, it is important to use the patient's name and to address any specific concerns or questions they raised in their initial email. Provide relevant information, answer common questions, and make it easy for them to schedule an appointment or ask questions.

Just like with social media, make sure the email is written in a friendly and professional tone. Include clear and concise contact info, such as the practice's phone number and email address, so the potential patient can easily contact the practice if they have further questions.

You want to make sure you or your staff respond promptly, ideally within twenty-four hours of receiving the email. This shows the potential patient that the practice values their time and is committed to providing exceptional service. Even if an answer cannot be provided promptly, reception of their email should be acknowledged immediately.

Phone communication

Optimize the initial phone call with a potential new patient by having a script or guidelines in place that cover important information such as the practice's services, hours of operation, and location.

Train your staff on active listening, empathy, and verbal and nonverbal communication so that they are able to communicate effectively with prospective patients.

Staff should also be prepared to answer common questions and provide information on the patient's next steps, such as scheduling an appointment.

A positive, personalized, and efficient initial phone conversation can create a great first impression and increase the likelihood of converting prospects into actual patients.

Provide seamless and personalized communications

This can include providing personalized responses to email and phone inquiries, and using chatbots or virtual assistants to provide instant answers to common questions. By personalizing communications and providing tailored information, you build trust and begin to establish a relationship with them, increasing the likelihood of converting them into actual patients. Anticipating the patient's needs and fulfilling them before they are expressed always goes a long way to create an exceptional experience.

Measure and manage first contact

Measuring and managing the initial contact with ideal prospects can be done by gathering feedback from potential patients, monitoring the effectiveness of marketing and communication strategies, and analyzing patient data to identify patterns and trends.

You can then identify areas for improvement and make changes to ensure they are effectively attracting and retaining their ideal potential patients.

"Wow" is what comes to mind. Super warm welcome, not like what you would expect from a medical office. The doctor's assistant and the surgeon were amazing. The consultation was almost an hour, but I did not feel rushed. The receptionist was awesome and super helpful to plan my surgery. Hotel recommendations and even recommendations for dining in Montreal.

Action Step

What three ways can you enhance your onboarding process with potential new patients?

1. _____

_____

_____

_____

2. _____

_____

_____

_____

3. _____

_____

_____

_____

Notes

14

Design a Facility for Relaxation and Healing

"We see our customers as invited guests to a party, and we are the hosts. It's our job every day to make every important aspect of the customer experience a little bit better."

—JEFF BEZOS

The physical environment of a healthcare practice plays a significant role in the patient experience. A welcoming and comfortable environment can help reduce anxiety and promote relaxation, which can lead to improved patient outcomes.

In this chapter, we will discuss how to design a facility that promotes relaxation and healing and how to incorporate amenities that enhance the patient experience, drawing inspiration from the hospitality and entertainment industries.

As in the hospitality industry, the design of a healthcare facility will have a major impact on the patient experience. First impressions matter, and last impressions, well, are lasting. To create a welcoming and comfortable environment, it's important to consider factors such as lighting, color, and layout.

Lighting

Natural light is best for a healthcare facility because it helps reduce anxiety and promote relaxation. Large windows and skylights can be used to bring natural light into the facility, similar to a hotel room with floor-to-ceiling windows for natural light and views.

If you don't have access to natural light in your lobby, there are still several ways to create a bright and welcoming atmosphere:

- **Artificial lighting** can create a warm and welcoming atmosphere. Choose fixtures that provide soft and diffused light rather than harsh or overly bright lighting.
- **Mirrors** can reflect light and create the illusion of more space and light in a room. Place large mirrors strategically around the lobby to reflect available natural or artificial light.
- **Plants** strategically placed in your lobby can not only add a touch of nature, but also help purify the air and create a more relaxed atmosphere. Plants can also create the illusion of natural light and a welcoming atmosphere.

Overall, there are many creative ways to brighten a lobby without natural light, and a combination of these techniques can create a warm, inviting, and comfortable environment.

Color

Color can have a major impact on the patient experience. Use light-colored walls and furniture to create a bright and airy feeling in the space. Pale shades of white, beige, or light blue can help create a soothing and calming effect. Soothing colors such as blue, green, and beige can be used to promote relaxation, similar to how a spa or wellness center would use neutral colors to create a peaceful atmosphere. Bright colors can be used to create a cheerful and uplifting environment, similar to how an amusement park uses bright colors to create an exciting atmosphere.

Scent

Using pleasant scents in a healthcare facility can greatly enhance the patient experience. Just as hotels use pleasant scents in their lobbies to create a welcoming atmosphere, healthcare clinics can use pleasant scents in common areas such as waiting rooms and reception areas to create a more relaxing environment for patients.

The use of essential oils or diffusers can be an effective way to introduce pleasant scents into the facility. For example, lavender oil is known for its calming properties, which can help reduce anxiety, while lemon oil is known for its refreshing properties, which can help promote a sense of well-being. In addition, pleasant scents can be used in specific areas of the clinic, such as treatment rooms, to create a more soothing atmosphere for patients.

It's important to note that it's always best to use natural and unscented products, as some patients may have allergies or sensitivities to certain scents.

DESIGN A FACILITY FOR RELAXATION AND HEALING

Layout

The layout of a healthcare facility affects the patient experience. Consider factors such as accessibility, privacy, and traffic flow, similar to how a theme park or shopping mall would consider traffic flow and accessibility for guests.

Include amenities that enhance the patient experience.

In addition to the physical design of the facility, amenities can enhance the patient experience, similar to how the entertainment industry provides amenities for its guests. Some amenities that can be incorporated include the following.

- [ ] **Comfortable seating**

    Patients may be in the facility for an extended period of time, so comfortable seating is important, similar to how a movie theater or concert venue would provide comfortable seating for guests. Use colorful accents such as throw pillows and rugs to create a lively and cheerful atmosphere.

- [ ] **Entertainment**

    Patients may appreciate having access to entertainment such as televisions, books, and magazines, similar to how a hotel room would provide a television and in-room entertainment for guests.

    Hang artwork with bright and vibrant colors to stimulate the visual senses and imagination.

- [ ] **Internet access**

    Patients may appreciate having access to the Internet while in the facility. Make the Wi-Fi access code easily accessible and the process of getting online seamless.

- [ ] **Food and beverage**

    Being in a hospital or other healthcare facility can be stressful and challenging for patients and their family members, and having access to food and beverages can help provide a sense of normalcy and comfort. Providing food and beverages can help patients feel more comfortable and at home during their stay. Your patients will appreciate it.

    Include a bowl of seasonal fruit such as apples, bananas, oranges, grapes, chocolates, and baked goods such as muffins, scones, or comforting cookies to delight your patients while waiting for their appointment.

    A cooler of bottled water can be a refreshing and convenient option for patients who may be feeling dehydrated. Lemon or cucumber water will add a special zest to the experience.

- [ ] **Special needs accommodations**

    It is important to consider the needs of patients with special needs, such as wheelchair accessibility.

If one could envision having surgery as a good time, this place is it! One could not be more relaxed in the operating room: my choice of music (smooth jazz) and a light show (no kidding) go a long way to making this surgical experience unique, relaxed, and memorable. Dr. Brutus and his team want to make sure that you not only have expert medical attention and treatment, but also a really great experience! I'm so grateful to everyone there! Thank you so much!

DESIGN A FACILITY FOR RELAXATION AND HEALING

Action Step

What three ways can you redesign your facility to make your patients feel at home?

1. _____

2. _____

3. _____

Notes

15

Develop Exceptional Communication Skills and Personalized Care

"If you want to lift yourself up, lift up someone else."

—BOOKER T. WASHINGTON

Patient outcomes depend on successful communication. But more than that, your relationship with your patients will be most affected by your communication skills. In fact, nothing affects the patient experience more than your communication skills.

If you are not willing to work on this, stop reading the book! Relax, it is not hard. Just follow these principles and you will be golden.

Speak to be understood

Speak the patient's language. Don't assume they understand complex medical jargon. They don't. And when people don't understand you, it creates distance. Use simple words. Make things easy to understand.

Imagine you are talking to a family member who knows nothing about medicine. If they happen to speak another language, try to say a few words in their language if you can. If you can't, then ask, "How do you say hello in your language?" This will go a long way toward establishing an immediate rapport with your patient. You can never go wrong with genuine interest!

Master body language

Patients often feel rushed in the doctor's office. One way to make them feel heard and not rushed is to look them in the eye while you answer questions. Writing or reviewing notes, checking your phone, or performing a physical exam while talking to the patient will speed things up, but it will feel more transactional to the patient.

The physical language you speak is as important, if not more important, than the words you use. Your posture, facial expressions, and tone of voice all affect your communication. Be aware of your posture. Use a relaxed, open posture (arms open, legs relaxed). A friendly tone will make you approachable and encourage conversation.

Don't just talk with compassion. *Act* with compassion.

Connect and get personal

If you want to build a relationship with your patients, every encounter should feel personal. Use their names when you speak to them. Review their chart information before you enter the room. Prepare to make a great impression!

Make notes in the chart of any pertinent information, such as the names of caregivers attending the appointment and any significant life events, such as birthdays or anniversaries, and incorporate these details into your conversation. The patient will appreciate being remembered, and the appointment will feel more personal.

A friendly and reassuring hand on the patient's shoulder or arm goes a long way toward making the patient feel like a person. Use their name several times during your interaction with them. Ask general questions about their life, family, and work, and return to these questions at future visits.

Listen actively

Active listening shifts your focus from what is going on in your head to your patient's needs. It also builds trust and establishes rapport. Use nonverbal cues to show that you are truly giving undivided attention. Lean in, nod, and make eye contact frequently. Ask open-ended questions and paraphrase to show you understand. Ask: "Am I understanding you correctly?"

Be likable

Being friendly and warm puts patients at ease, builds or maintains trust, and is likely to lead to more open discussions and higher compliance rates. Patients rate friendliness and humanity in a doctor as more important than competence! Remember that performance is part of professionalism. Perform for your patient like an actor on a stage. In other words, embody the role you have chosen. After all, you are an important actor on the stage of their lives.

Show confidence but not overconfidence

It is important to be confident in your interactions with patients. After all, they come to you with uncertainty, fear, or concern. Nothing says "run away" like a doctor who does not seem to know what he is saying or doing. But be careful not to appear overly confident, cocky, or arrogant. There is no room for arrogance, narcissism, or condescension in your relationship with your patient. A good way to ensure that you are not perceived as arrogant is to give genuine compliments. There is always something to like about every person you meet. Look for it and compliment them sincerely.

Show and speak with empathy

Treat the person, not the disease or condition. Get to know the person by asking questions. Be interested. Pay attention to signs of emotion expressed by your patients. You cannot respond to what you do not recognize. Pay attention to facial expressions, tone of voice, and other nonverbal cues. Sit next to your patient, not across the desk or standing. Smile at them, not while they speak. Touch them as you would a friend. This is a very vulnerable relationship. Honor it. Cherish it. Express your concern for them. You are helping a person in pain. Remember that. The more you practice acting with empathy, the more natural it will become.

Be open-minded and respectful

People will be more open to communicating with you if you show respect for them and their beliefs. Patients come in all colors and flavors, with different social and cultural backgrounds. They have different beliefs and cultures that affect the patient's perspective. You want them to feel understood, valued, and validated. Show interest and genuine curiosity about their own understanding and perceptions. Avoid being judgmental or dismissive.

End with a few questions

At the end of your session, stop and ask your patient:

- Do you feel comfortable with the treatments we discussed?
- Do you have any concerns about our approach?
- What else would you like to know about your condition?
- What other concerns do you have?

This final opportunity to address the patient's concerns will help the patient feel much more comfortable. As always, remember that what is not measured is not treated. So…

During my initial consultation, the surgeon took the time to thoroughly explain the procedure and answer all of my questions. He was patient, kind, and understanding, which helped to alleviate any anxiety I had about the surgery.

On the day of the procedure, the surgeon and his team . . . made sure I was comfortable and informed throughout the entire process, which made a huge difference in my overall experience.

Following the surgery, he was diligent about my post-operative care, ensuring that I had all the necessary resources and information to heal properly. He was available to answer any questions or concerns I had and followed up with me regularly to monitor my progress.

Thanks to the skillful hands of this incredible surgeon, I am now able to use my joint pain-free, and my quality of life has improved tremendously. Their expertise, professionalism, and genuine care for their patients are unparalleled, and I am truly grateful for their exceptional work.

Action Step

Given the concepts presented in this chapter, what are three ways you can modify your communication approach or techniques to better connect with and support your patients?

1. _____

2. _____

3. _____

Notes

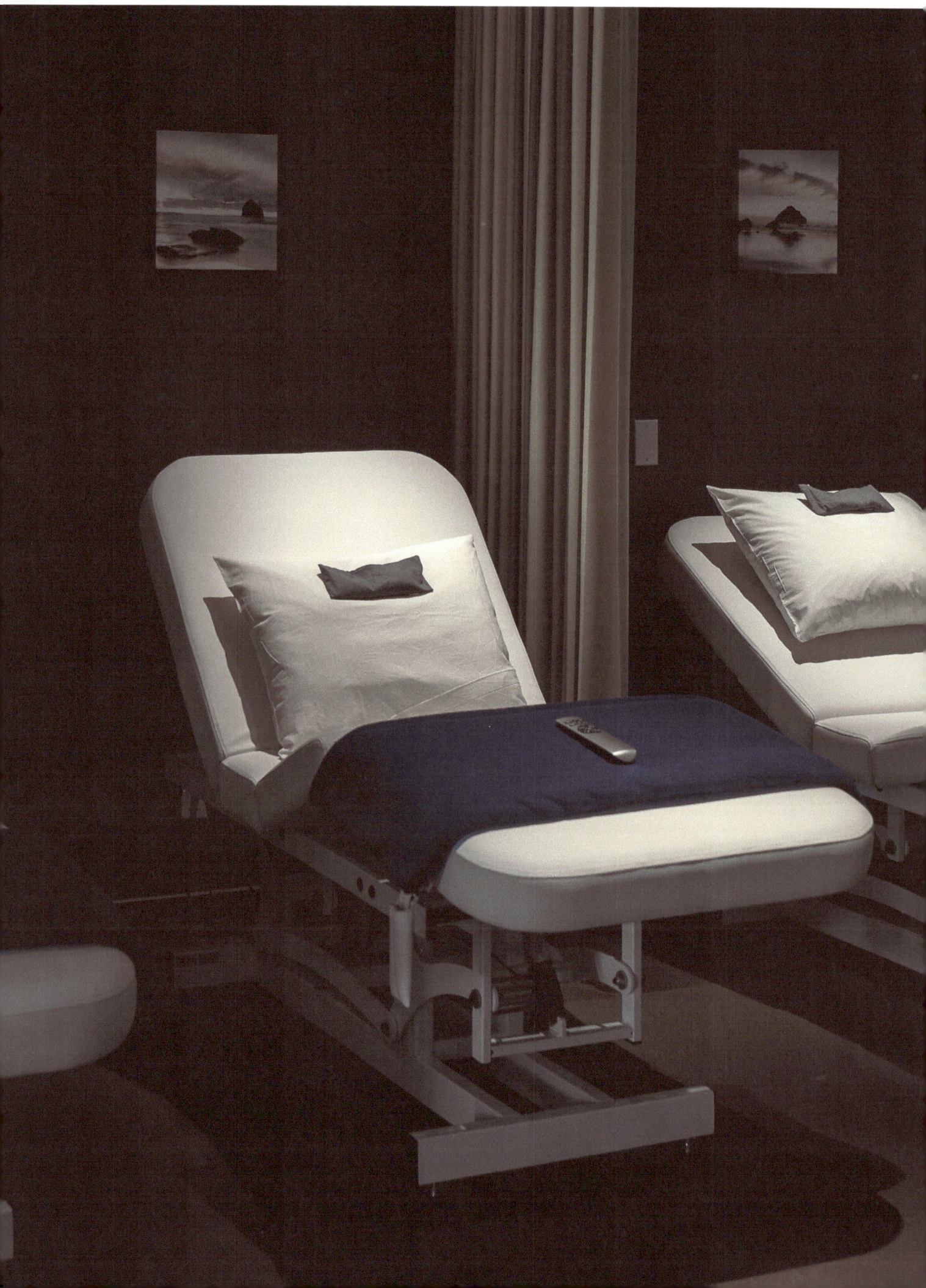

16

Elevate Patient Expectations

"Blessed is he who expects nothing, for he shall never be disappointed."

—ALEXANDER POPE

Truly understanding the patient's expectations, ideas, and concerns on an exceptional level is critical to success, and too often busy physicians assume that the patient simply wants to get better.

Identifying patient expectations

Strangely, this topic is rarely taught in medical school or even during residency. In fact, it is quite logical for patients and physicians to see things differently, both in terms of knowledge and perspective.

Every physician with a few gray hairs has painful memories of poorly understanding what their patient wanted from the interaction with them.

Of course, for certain conditions, such as an acute infection, the patient wants and expects to be treated and to heal quickly with appropriate treatment, and often, thanks to the tremendous advances in medicine, it is possible to achieve the expected outcome.

For a chronic condition, however, the assumptions of the physician and the patient can be very different.

As much as the patient-physician relationship is a two-way street and more of a partnership than in the era of paternalistic medicine (the doctor just knew best and the patient went along), the responsibility for identifying and managing the patient's expectations rests on the shoulders of the physician.

Expectations may or may not be realistic, and they may or may not be expressed. If you want to achieve what the patient would define as success, there is no way around it. You have to ask. If not, you are playing "pin the tail on the donkey" with a blindfold.

Consider incorporating these questions into your interactions with them:

- What would you like me to do for you today?
- What result are you looking for?
- How would you define success?
- What would have to happen for you to say that this consultation or treatment was a success?
- What do you think is the best way to proceed?
- Do you have any thoughts on how we should handle this issue today?

Patients also have ideas about what is wrong with them. They have often been thinking about it for a while and have probably done some research. Sometimes a lot of research. As such, an important part of their expectations is being listened to, so you should take that into account.

Questions like these can be very powerful for gaining insight, but also for eliciting what they expect from their encounter with you:

- Do you have any ideas about what is causing this problem?
- Do you have any theories about what is happening?
- I think it would be useful for me to hear your thoughts on this. Can you help me?

Finally, patients have concerns that they may not bring to your attention unless you ask about them. It is important to bring them up early and certainly before they materialize. That would be the wrong time to find out about them!

- What is your biggest concern or worry about what this problem might be?
- Are you worried about this situation being anything in particular?
- What is the worst thing that you think this could be?
- What is your dominant worry about this problem?

When your patient opens up and begins to talk about their expectations, ideas, and concerns, listen, encourage, and show empathy and understanding.

It is not the time to manage them (yet). Listen and get to know your patient.

Managing patients' unrealistic expectations

Patients and professionals may have different expectations about how the care experience should be delivered. Expectations may be related to the outcomes of clinical care or to non-clinical aspects. This is even more true as the COVID-19 pandemic exacerbated limitations on the number of patients that can be seen and treated, for example due to staff shortages or delays and backlogs.

Patients are becoming consumers as they pay more for their care, even in countries that pride themselves on having universal healthcare systems, such as Canada. Naturally, as patients foot more of the healthcare bill, their expectations rise.

Expectations come in many flavors and can be expressed or not, reasonable or not.

Factors that can cause patients to have unrealistic expectations include the following.

- **Inadequate information**

  Patients may not have received enough education or information in terms they can easily understand about what to expect, the wait times, availability of staff and resources, or possible complications of treatment. Each patient is different and will have different needs and levels of understanding. Jargon and acronyms should be avoided. Sometimes, and when appropriate, a companion may be included in the conversation to reduce the risk of omission or confusion.

- **Too much information**

  Patients today are more knowledgeable and sophisticated in their healthcare relationships than any other time in history. Too much information can also lead to unrealistic expectations based on misinformation, past experiences, and stories told by friends and acquaintances whose situations may have been different. Time spent with the patient is necessary to listen, understand, and correct their understanding of their condition if required. You cannot do that correctly with only five minutes of facetime.

- **Not enough time**

  Time is a growing concern as pandemic-related measures have increased the burden on staff to keep patients and staff safe. Providing adequate information to all patients before they undergo treatment now takes more time, as medical care has become more of a partnership between doctor and patient than in the days of more paternalistic forms of medical care.

- **Anxiety and misunderstandings**

  Anxiety can interfere with the process of properly educating the patient and increase the risk of unspoken misunderstandings. Don't hesitate to ask your patient what they want from their consultation or treatment. Don't assume they will tell you they didn't understand or fully comprehend what you explained. Let them ask more questions.

  Show empathy and understanding. Exceptional medical care is based on exceptional rapport and relationships that lead to exceptional trust between the patient and their doctor.

- **Leaning too much on the system**

  The most important part of a patient-centered practice is putting the patient's needs first, not the system's.

To achieve this result, a culture must be created, and it is critical that leadership puts its own people first and, paradoxically, patients second. This is no easy task because most healthcare organizations, large and small, are set in their ways, and in most cases, those ways are outdated.

Restructure the system to ensure that patient preferences and convenience are at the center of every practice process.

Management is responsible for building the culture. If you do this part right, the front-line staff who interact with patients will deliver the experience you design. In other words, when management takes great care of their people, the people will take great care of patients.

After all, they are the ones who will handle most of the expectations, as many questions or comments will be made after the consultation or procedure—and these are not necessarily directed at the treating professional.

Getting your team on board with this change is imperative, but not easy. Resistance to change is human. Aligning the staff to this culture with the goal of patient satisfaction requires strong leadership because the practice must be redesigned. It is likely that some staff will be unable or unwilling to adapt to this new culture and will need to be replaced.

Your team will need to understand that patients are the lifeblood of your practice and that they are human beings with feelings. Furthermore, like most people, their decisions will be influenced more by their desires and emotions than by their rational thoughts. Needless to say, the patient's perspective will be very important to the practice's bottom line.

Reviewing existing processes

A review of existing processes will be necessary with this perspective in mind, including:

- **Scheduling and office hours**
  Convenience is a major differentiator for today's patients. The less specialized your practice is, the more convenient it should be for your patients. Are you offering virtual visits? Safe and confidential digital communication?

- **In-office patient experience**
  A seamless experience, demonstrating respect for the patient's time, informing them about delays and realistic scheduling will make a significant impact on your patient experience.

- **Billing, payment options, and collections**
  Make it easy to pay for your services, be creative to make your services accessible, and provide peace of mind to your patients with price transparency.

☐ Streamline insurance processing

Before providing medical services to a patient, verify the patient's insurance coverage, and eligibility for your services in advance to help you avoid claim denials or payment delays. Submit accurate claims to the insurance company, and be sure to include all required information on the claim (patient's diagnosis, treatment codes, and any required supporting documentation). Using electronic claims submission is faster and more efficient than paper-based claims submission. Most insurance companies now accept electronic claims, which can help you get paid faster and reduce the risk of errors.

If a claim is not paid within a set timeframe, follow up immediately with the insurance company to determine the reason for the delay. This can help you identify any issues that need to be addressed and ensure that you get paid for your services.

If you are not getting paid in a timely manner, negotiate contracts with insurance companies to ensure that you are fairly compensated for your services and address any issues related to claims processing or payment delays. Consider dropping insurance and moving to a cash-based practice if issues keep piling up.

☐ Customer service efficiency

Consider that your patients are customers and treat them accordingly, with respect and with consideration for their efforts, time, and trust. Empathetic and compassionate staff will create magic.

☐ Referral practices

A well-optimized referral process will significantly improve patient experience and outcomes. Your referral process should be easy to navigate and understand for both patients and referring providers. Some tips:

- Ensure that the process is well-documented and communicated to patients in a clear and concise manner.
- Use technology, such as electronic referral systems, to automate the process, reduce errors, and save time for everyone involved.
- Ensure that patients are promptly notified of their referral status and next steps.
- Keep referring providers in the loop by providing timely updates on the patient's progress and any test results. This improves the patient experience by reducing anxiety and uncertainty.
- Encourage collaboration and communication between referring providers and specialists.
- Offer support to patients who may have difficulty navigating the process or accessing care. Monitor and improve the referral process regularly. Use patient feedback on the referral process and patient experience.

Exceeding patient expectations

Once you have identified what they are, start creating a culture (your people) and implementing systems (your how) that will allow you to consistently meet your patients' expectations. The key to progress is consistency. You want to avoid hits and misses.

You want a high batting average.

Once you and your team achieve consistency, you can get fancy and start exceeding expectations, if you so choose. The best way to exceed expectations, much like the Ritz Carlton does, is to create memorable moments or wow stories. Here are some tips on how to do just that.

☐ **Surprise them**

Yes, use the element of surprise, and do it with something they can't possibly expect. It can be a gift, a handwritten note signed by the doctor, a birthday card, or even a souvenir picture with their favorite doctor. It can be anything you can think of, as long as it is thoughtful and, most importantly, unexpected.

☐ **Improve your response time**

We live in a world of convenience and fast service. Patients will compare your services to every other non-healthcare business, even retail. Hello, Amazon! As a result, they are now accustomed to quick responses to emails or phone calls. They also want to be helped efficiently. So, don't send them to generic FAQ pages, because that won't work. Direct them to the answer they are looking for. Today's customers and patients want to do as little work as possible to get the solution they are looking for. It is called convenience, and they are willing to pay a premium to those who deliver it.

Remember I mentioned Amazon Prime earlier in the book? In case you need further reminders, Amazon makes an additional $25 billion yearly just from Prime services! Because faster is better.

Showing them that you care more about their needs than your own will give them compelling reasons to trust you and do business with you.

☐ **Deliver a seamless experience across channels**

This will be a challenge for healthcare companies and practices due to confidentiality issues. However, patients can now reach out to your medical office or practice through social media like Instagram, Facebook, or direct messaging and chat. When they move to a phone conversation, they will appreciate and even expect not to have to start their story from scratch.

Be mindful of these modern ways, and be creative with technology and systems so you don't lose the valuable information they provide before they get more personal with you.

ELEVATE PATIENT EXPECTATIONS

Do not forget to document the communication exchanges in the patient's medical file, to comply with the requirements of your medical or professional boards.

☐ Don't kill promises

Trust is a precious currency. Once broken or lost, it is difficult to repair or replace. Do not make promises you cannot keep just to appear competitive.

Be careful with your words. A word is a promise in today's world, and patients tend to be less forgiving. Underpromise and overdeliver, and you will be fine.

☐ Get personal and anticipate

Patients, like any modern consumer, want a personalized experience that is tailored to their preferences.

Use their names, as the gesture builds trust and respect. Ever been to a Starbucks? There's a reason Starbucks employees ask for your name so they can spell it wrong on your coffee cup. Hell, you now have a "Starbucks name." It's a thing! Is that genius or what?

Mine is Jaypee.

Being thoughtful and anticipating your patients' needs before they mention them will help you build a reputation as a patient-centered practice and foster long-lasting relationships. Medicine, just like business, is relationship-building and nurturing.

☐ Reward loyalty

Get creative with ways to show your frequent fliers you appreciate them. Everyone likes to feel special. Patients certainly do. Offer them treats, flowers, a thank-you card, or a special reward for their loyalty or referrals. Make sure you do it ethically and in accordance with the rules of your professional associations. Keep in touch with them. Let them know you think of them before they think of you. Use technology and send them personalized content to strengthen the relationship.

Meeting and exceeding your patients' expectations is no longer optional, especially if you're in private practice. Going the extra mile to meet your patients' physical and emotional needs will pay off in more ways than just financially.

Dr. Brutus, thank you for your empathy, compassion, kindness; these values are unparalleled within you and therefore reflect within your team. As I've already mentioned in one of my follow-up appointments, those two surgeries were my best medical experiences; they were not simply surgeries, they were life experiences so warm and so rewarding! You have an innate sense of putting your patients at ease from the first meeting. You are offering a service of the highest quality, and I felt in very good hands and secure from our first appointment.

Action Step

What three expectations have you noticed your patients have, and what have done (or can further elevate) to address them?

1. _____

_____

_____

_____

2. _____

_____

_____

_____

3. _____

_____

_____

_____

17

Optimize the Physical Exam

"Of all the gifts we can give to people, the gift of our touch is one of the most priceless. Through our hands we convey a kind of radiance. A warmth seeps out from our inner fire, a wrap for someone's chill, a light for another's dark."

—JAN PHILLIPS

Besides being heard, being examined by you, the physician or practitioner, is the reason they come to you in the first place. In other words, patients want to be examined. They want you to look at them physically, to find out what's wrong or out of place, and will be disappointed if you don't.

The physical examination is a crucial part of the patient-doctor relationship because it conveys a special sense of caring to patients, who often report feeling much better after a physical examination. This in itself is an important therapeutic effect that should not be underestimated. Don't miss this opportunity.

Expectations

Understanding patient expectations for the physical examination is essential to providing a superior and compassionate patient experience.

Remember that the healthcare environment is familiar to you, but not to your patient. As a result, any physical event, such as a procedure or even a physical examination, can feel strange and even upsetting.

Professionalism, respect, kindness, and a sense of rapport or connection are essential to an exceptional patient experience.

Set the stage

Take the time to make your patient feel comfortable. And let them know it.

Use phrases such as "Please make yourself comfortable" or "I want you to feel comfortable at all times. If there is anything that makes you uncomfortable, please let me know." That will allow you to express your concern. Don't assume they know you're concerned; tell them. Make sure they know.

Protect their privacy and dignity

Allow your patient to undress privately in a separate room or behind a curtain. At the very least, turn or look away so they feel less exposed as they undress. Be mindful of cultural differences.

Provide them with a gown or other appropriate cover for the examination,

They are used to seeing naked bodies and exposed body parts. But they are not. And that is the key here.

Show that you are worthy of the privilege

Remember that being touched by you is a privilege that patients grant you, the practitioner, because they trust you. It should be done in a way that expresses your concern for their sense of safety, comfort, privacy, and dignity. Note that I said "expresses" because if it is not expressed, it may not be perceived by your patient.

Too many physicians assume that their patients know what is going to happen during the physical examination and rush through the steps without enough consideration for the human experience from the patient's perspective.

Explain what you are going to do

Don't rush through the exam like a robot. You are examining a human being who is in a very vulnerable position, often undressed. Let them know what you are going to do so they are prepared. Preparedness reduces anxiety, addresses control issues, and allows your patient to understand and be an active participant in the examination rather than a passive party.

Ask permission, as it's polite

Be courteous and ask permission to perform the necessary examination. Don't assume that the patient has given permission just because he or she is in your office.

Also, ask permission to have a student or trainee present in the room. It will make your patient feel respected. And in most cases, if they are properly informed (and asked), they will be more than happy to contribute to the education of the next generation.

Apologize, and show you care

Some aspects of a physical examination can be uncomfortable or even painful. You know this because you've done it, but your patient doesn't. Let them know before you hurt them, not after. Apologize for causing pain, even if it is sometimes unavoidable. It is not about you, it is about making them feel respected.

Use phrases like:

- I know this is a little (or a lot) uncomfortable.
- I am sorry to have to do this to you.
- This will only be uncomfortable for a moment.
- Let me know if I need to stop at any time, OK?
- Is there anything I can do to make you more comfortable?

Use a chaperone whom the patient can trust

If necessary, use a chaperone. Ideally, someone the patient trusts. A chaperone can be a healthcare professional or even a trained, unlicensed staff member, such as a physician's assistant, nurse, technician, or therapist.

The chaperone acts as a witness for the patient and the healthcare professional during a medical examination or procedure.

Ideally, the chaperone should be of the gender with which the patient is most comfortable, depending on the nature of the examination, and may be of particular interest for sensitive examinations.

Be aware that a patient's personal and cultural preferences may expand their own definition of a sensitive examination.

Limit conversation

At least when they are naked! Don't talk too much while they are undressed. Believe me, they are not listening and are more focused on being uncomfortable. Let them get dressed or at least covered properly before you talk to them.

Remember, whatever the physical examination maneuver is, it is familiar to you but not to your patient.

Dr. Brutus is a rockstar and his staff are the best I've ever met. They went above and beyond to fix my finger, which he immediately noted still had glass in the wound from my accident over a month before. He booked me for an immediate surgery and had the glass and scar tissue removed. That instantly restored my finger, which had been completely immobilized for thirty days. After a brief post-surgery recovery period and a few follow-ups, they made sure I was comfortable, and the pain medication was sufficient. It's been a month since the surgery, and I'm off the hard medication already. 5/5 stars!

Action Step

What three ways can you identify where you can elevate the examination experience?

1. _____

_____

_____

_____

2. _____

_____

_____

_____

3. _____

_____

_____

_____

18

Elevate the Diagnostic and Surgical Experiences

"I become faint and nauseous during even minor medical procedures, such as making an appointment by phone."

—DAVE BARRY

The diagnostic experience

Undergoing diagnostic tests is stressful for patients. Some diagnostic procedures are uncomfortable or even painful.

Patients are often unsure what to expect and may be stressed by the results.

Interacting with a patient who is about to undergo a medical test provides you with a unique opportunity to make a difference by demonstrating empathy and caring.

Think of a diagnostic procedure as an opportunity to improve the patient experience. Seize it!

Here are some strategies to help you make the difference that makes a difference.

Ask about and validate your patient's feelings, and offer support and empathy throughout the process. Encourage them to share their concerns and fears.

Do not assume the patient knows anything about the test, and explaining the test before it happens will help reduce anxiety. Help them understand what will happen, what they will feel, and why it is necessary.

Use clear, concise language. Avoid jargon. Keep it simple. This will make the experience less intimidating.

Reduce wait times for diagnostic results so you can begin treatment promptly, which is important to patients.

Use better and less invasive technology and calming methods to reduce anxiety and pain or discomfort associated with diagnostic procedures, such as quieter machines, soothing colors or scents. Aromatherapy and spa-like music can work wonders.

Keep your patient and family informed as needed. Provide regular updates and feedback during the diagnostic process, and involve the patient in decision-making whenever possible to build trust and improve the patient experience.

Support your patient through the process and validate their feelings. Offer empathy and compassion to reduce stress and improve your patient's experience.

The surgical experience

No one wants to have surgery. But you may need it. Having surgery is a stressful experience for most people. The feelings a patient will have about it have a lot to do with their personal past experiences, the type of surgery being performed and, of course, their individual circumstances.

While surgery is rarely considered fun by the patient, it is possible to make the experience more enjoyable by focusing on the patient's experience rather than just the technical aspects of the procedure.

Here is a list of tips and tricks you can use to make your surgical patient experience exceptional.

- Provide clear and thorough information about the procedure and postoperative care so that the patient and their support system (family or significant others) know what to expect and can make informed decisions.

- Explain potential risks and complications and discuss ways to reduce, minimize, or manage these risks.

- Actively elicit and listen to the patient's concerns and answer questions in a way that is easy to understand.

- Involve the patient in the decision making process and, to the extent possible, allow the patient to choose the type of sedation, anxiolysis, and anesthesia.

- Offer a preoperative tour of the hospital or surgical facility to help the patient feel more familiar and comfortable with the environment.

- Encourage local anesthesia when possible to avoid the need for fasting before surgery, which can cause dizziness and fainting.

- Use gentler, less invasive techniques whenever possible to minimize pain and discomfort.

- Provide clean and comfortable rooms in which to await surgery, as well as spotless and aesthetically pleasing surgical facilities.

ELEVATE THE DIAGNOSTIC AND SURGICAL EXPERIENCES

- Provide comfortable and attractive surgical gowns or scrubs to wear during the procedure and maintain their modesty. No one likes a hospital gown.

- Offer amenities such as access to entertainment, technology, or supportive care services to distract the patient and reduce anxiety.

- Allow the patient to choose the music in the operating or procedure room. It's about them, remember?

- Teach your patient breathing and relaxation techniques to reduce anxiety.

- Engage and reassure your patient during the procedure if it is being performed under local anesthesia on a wide-awake patient, or use technology such as virtual reality to help your patient become distracted or relaxed through an immersive experience.

- Provide support and resources to help your patient prevent and manage pain after the procedure.

- Provide access to pain management specialists or other care providers as needed to manage post-surgical discomfort.

- Anticipate and meet their needs before they are expressed.

- Provide written, verbal, and educational videos to educate your patients about their postoperative care and help them manage their recovery.

- Offer patients a variety of delicious and nutritious food options during their stay to help them feel better and maintain their well-being.

- Provide frequent follow-up check-ins to monitor the patient's recovery and address any concerns or complications early.

- Take a patient-centered approach and focus on the individual needs of each patient to improve the overall experience.

- Allow your patient to bring a supportive friend or family member to the hospital or surgical facility for emotional support.

- Offer patients access to support groups and online communities where they can connect with others who have undergone the same type of procedure.

- Encourage patients to share their feelings and emotions with the team and provide support and guidance as needed.

- Encourage patients to maintain a positive attitude and sense of humor, and offer support and encouragement throughout the surgical process.

- Involve the patient in their own care by encouraging them to ask questions, make decisions, and take an active role in their recovery.

- Provide the patient with a detailed plan for postoperative care, including information about diet, medications, follow-up appointments, and activity restrictions.
- Provide the patient with information about support services and resources, such as housing and financial assistance for transportation.
- Recognize and celebrate the patient's progress and accomplishments during recovery.
- Use patient feedback and experience surveys to let patients know you care and to identify areas for potential improvement and optimization of their experience.

I've listened with great interest to your interview on YouTube, where you say you prefer a practice that is based on the quality and value of the relationship established with each person, and it shows. We the patients feel it! I have actually received a lot more than I expected, even a chocolate cupcake!

Thank you for Eugene and Eugénie!
I'm taking good care of them!

Thank you for the chocolate cupcake!

Dr. Brutus, you are one in a million!

Action Step

Based on what you've read in this chapter, what three ways can you elevate either the diagnostic experience or surgical experience?

1. _____

2. _____

3. _____

Notes

PART 3

Important Tips for Creating Exceptional Patient Experiences

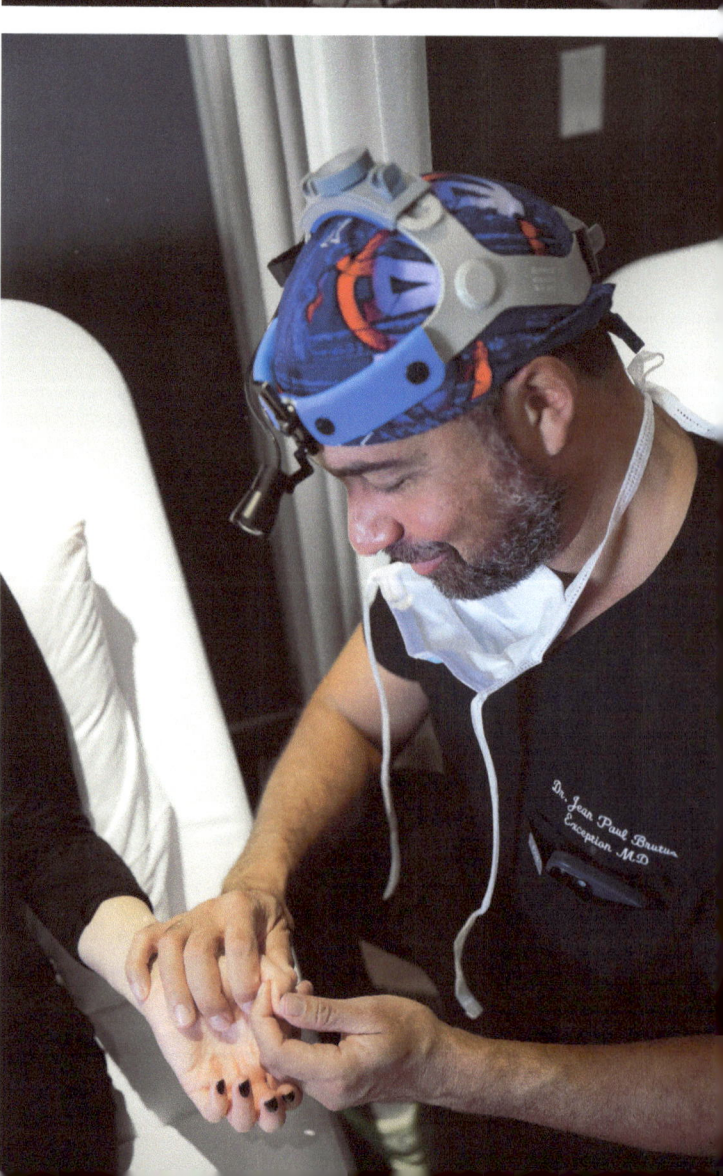

19

Make Lasting Impressions by Creating Memorable Moments and Stories

"The customer's perception is your reality."

—KATE ZABRISKIE

I have always been fascinated by the fact that many of my patients have been operated on by other surgeons, but cannot even remember their names. How is this possible?

You see, people only remember what went really badly or what went exceptionally well. If their expectations are barely met, they simply don't remember.

If you want to create lasting impressions, you have to create moments worth remembering.

Creating memorable moments and stories is a key aspect of elevating the patient experience from ordinary to extraordinary. It is something that healthcare providers can learn from the hospitality and entertainment industries, where making a positive and lasting impression on customers is essential.

One effective way to create memorable moments and stories is to personalize the patient experience. This can be done by taking the time to get to know patients on a personal level and understand their individual needs and preferences.

Make notes

Make notes in the patient's record of anything they mention that will help you personalize your next interaction. If they mention it, it matters to them, so it should matter to you. Review the chart immediately before meeting with the patient and use the information to make the patient feel special, remembered, and cared for.

Create custom care

Create personalized care plans, tailored treatment options, and special accommodations that can make a big difference in the patient experience; for example, if a patient has special dietary needs or cultural preferences, be sure to tailor their treatment options accordingly. By tailoring the experience to each patient, you can make them feel valued and special.

Provide exceptional service

This includes not only the medical care provided, but also the customer service aspect of the patient experience. A dedicated patient liaison or health assistant can help with scheduling, insurance, and other administrative tasks, and a comprehensive patient portal can make it easy for patients to communicate with their healthcare team and access their medical records.

Anticipate and address patient needs

Anticipate and address patient needs before they are expressed. For example, if a patient is recovering from surgery and is unable to drive, arrange for a car service to take them home and to follow-up appointments. If your patient is traveling from home and needs a hotel, provide them with a list of hotel and restaurant recommendations near your facility before they ask. Go above and beyond to meet your patients' needs.

Make it convenient and easy

Convenience is a critical aspect of creating memorable moments for patients. Offer virtual consultations, telemedicine, and remote monitoring services to make healthcare more accessible, flexible, and convenient for patients. Patients love convenience, just like any other customer, and the healthcare industry is lagging behind. Seize the opportunity by becoming an early adopter. Don't be a laggard.

Make it interactive

Make the experience more interactive by involving patients in their care process, such as allowing them to participate in decision making or providing them with educational materials. By making patients active participants in their care, healthcare providers can empower them and create a sense of ownership over their health.

MAKE LASTING IMPRESSIONS BY CREATING MEMORABLE MOMENTS AND STORIES

Surprise and delight them

Provide unexpected surprises and delights that make your patients feel special, such as a thoughtful gift, a handwritten note, or a complimentary service. Take note of important events such as a birthday, anniversary, or graduation. Commemorate them with your patients. You will be amazed at how much important information patients will share about themselves, their lives, and what is important to them when you take the time to listen and show that you truly care.

By exceeding patient expectations, healthcare providers can make a positive and lasting impression. People may not remember a name, but they will always remember how you made them feel.

Dr. Brutus performed the minimally invasive carpal tunnel relief surgery a year and a half ago. The pain relief was immediate, the healing uneventful, and since then my hand feels completely normal. I will be grateful to Dr. Brutus forever as I got the runaround from the local health services that would have meant pain for several months longer.

MAKE LASTING IMPRESSIONS BY CREATING MEMORABLE MOMENTS AND STORIES

Action Step

What three ways can you anticipate your patient's needs or pleasantly surprise them with your attention to personal detail?

1. _____

_____

_____

_____

2. _____

_____

_____

_____

3. _____

_____

_____

_____

Notes

20

Resolve Issues with an Exceptional Service Recovery Plan

"Statistics suggest that when customers complain, business owners and managers ought to get excited about it. The complaining customer represents a huge opportunity for more business."

—ZIG ZIGLAR

In private healthcare, delivering exceptional patient experiences is critical to building trust and loyalty with patients. However, even with the best intentions and efforts, mistakes or problems can occur. In these situations, it is important to have a service recovery plan in place to address and resolve any issues and ensure that patients feel valued and respected.

Be proactive

The best way to handle service recovery is to be proactive and prevent problems from occurring in the first place. This can be achieved through regular communication with patients, proactive monitoring of service quality, and continuous improvement efforts.

Apologize sincerely

If a problem does occur, it is important to offer a sincere apology to the patient. A sincere apology can go a long way in showing the patient that the provider understands the problem and is committed to resolving it. An apology does not mean you did something wrong. It expresses empathy and compassion.

Investigate the problem

When a problem occurs, it is important to investigate the issue to understand the root cause and take steps to prevent it from happening in the future. When you are working on an issue, you are truly handling two issues: the one you see today and the one you are preventing tomorrow! Use today's mishap as a way to create a better tomorrow for all.

Communicate effectively

Clear and effective communication is critical to service recovery. Keep patients informed about the status of their issue and the steps being taken to resolve it. They will appreciate being kept in the loop. You would, wouldn't you?

Take ownership

Take ownership of the problem and do not blame others or make excuses. Blaming others never helped anyone. This shows that the healthcare provider is committed to finding a solution and taking responsibility for the problem. Responsibility does not mean guilt. It means accountability, and commitment to your cause. It means leadership.

Offer a solution

Offer a solution to the problem that addresses the patient's needs and concerns. This may include offering compensation, a refund, or a free service. Ask the patient how you can make it better for them. They may have a solution that you did not think of, and they will feel that you listened to them. Double whammy!

Follow up

Follow up with the patient after the problem has been resolved to make sure they are satisfied with the solution and that the problem has been completely resolved. If it has, it shows you care. If it hasn't, you will want to know! Anticipation is power.

Learn and improve

Service recovery is not only about solving the problem, it is also an opportunity to learn and improve. Use the feedback and information gathered to improve service and prevent similar problems in the future. Make tomorrow better than today, and certainly better than yesterday. The world will be a better place for all if you adopt this philosophy.

RESOLVE ISSUES WITH AN EXCEPTIONAL SERVICE RECOVERY PLAN

Action Step

What three problems have you encountered or mistakes you or your staff have made, and how can you make sure those experiences don't happen again?

1. _____

_____

_____

_____

2. _____

_____

_____

_____

3. _____

_____

_____

_____

Notes

21

How NOT to Create an Exceptional Experience

"My expectations were reduced to zero when I turned 21. Everything since then has been a bonus."

—STEPHEN W. HAWKING

Creating an exceptional patient experience isn't just about what you do, it's also about what you don't do. Let's explore common mistakes that private healthcare professionals make that can negatively impact the patient experience, and what to avoid in order to create an exceptional patient experience.

Not valuing patient time

Long wait times, delayed appointments, and poor punctuality can all contribute to a negative patient experience. To avoid this, make sure patients are seen on time, keep wait times to a minimum, and communicate clearly when delays occur. Let patients know that you value their time. It is just as valuable as yours. Doctors are notoriously late, and sometimes it is unavoidable, but most of the time, it is due to poor planning and scheduling.

Lack of clear communication

Patients need to understand their diagnosis, treatment options, and what to expect during their visit. To avoid this, ensure that patients receive clear, accurate, and easy-to-understand information throughout their visit. Ask and verify that the information has been received and understood. Patients sometimes avoid telling you that they did not understand your explanations because they are afraid, embarrassed, or afraid of taking up too much of your time.

Not valuing the patient's opinion and knowledge

Do not dismiss patients' opinions, beliefs, and knowledge. Patients today have a tremendous amount of information at their fingertips. They are also the ones most familiar with their bodies. Patients tell stories. They tell you what they have. They just don't always have the words. Listen to what they say and what they do not say. You will be able to get to the diagnosis quickly, using what they are telling you and what you know as a medical practitioner.

Think about music. What is music? It is notes separated by silence. Music without silence is not music. It is simply noise. This analogy is meant to help you understand how important it is to listen to the patient's silence as well. That is, what they are not saying. Someone wise once said: If you stop interrupting patients, they will actually tell you what their diagnosis is.

Being dismissive

Do not dismiss them. Often they have done their own research and do not want to feel disrespected. Listen to them and refrain from any kind of judgment (with your words or body posture). Watch your body language in particular. Most physicians are not skilled at this. Be different. Be aware.

Speaking gibberish

Don't speak the doctor's language. Speak their language so they can understand you without feeling you are dumbing it down for them; explain with clarity, not medical jargon. Don't use abbreviations. Use simple terms a child could understand. Make it very simple.

Not being present

Don't type on your computer while listening to them. They want your attention. They want and need you to look them in the eye. They understand the need for documentation, but they value the relationship more than your notes. Your notes are for you. They are useless to them. Remember that. Increase the time you spend looking into their eyes. Give them one of the most precious gifts—presence.

Being condescending

Don't patronize them. Paternalistic medicine is dead. Patients want to be partners with you in their care; they want to feel (not just know or suspect) that you care about their health; they need to feel that they are part of the decision-making process.

Be aware of your tone. It conveys a lot. Use a friendly and respectful tone that shows you care about their health. Encourage your patients to ask questions. This can help build trust and rapport with your patients.

Using visual aids, such as diagrams or pictures, will help your patients better understand their health condition or treatment options. It shows you truly care.

Being in a rush

Don't rush them. Patients want to be treated as people, not as time slots. Start your appointment on time so your patient doesn't feel like you're rushing through their appointment to make up for lost time. If you are going to be late, let them know ahead of time so they can adjust their schedules if necessary. Show empathy and listen carefully to your patient's concerns to make them feel heard and understood. Maintain good eye contact and avoid interrupting or rushing them while they are speaking.

When you are with your patients, try to focus only on them and avoid multitasking. Avoid checking your phone or computer. Show that you are engaged and attentive.

Schedule fewer patients for higher-quality consultations. Ask patients if they have any questions before ending the session. Always finish strong.

Disrespecting their work

Don't ask patients to repeat information they've already provided, such as their medical history. Prepare before you see them. More importantly, let them know you have prepared for them. Show them you already know them, or at least some of the information they have given you. Access to private information is a privilege.

Assuming

Don't assume that you know what your patient wants or prefers. Explain the different treatment options you are considering and ask them what they want or prefer. Your patients want options. Ask them why they would prefer this option. Assess expectations and make sure they are reasonable and can be met if you are aiming for success. You know the adage about when you assume....

Not being honest

Don't bullshit them. If you don't know, say so. Most people have a BS detector. Tell them that you will be working with another doctor who may be more specialized to find out what their problem is and what treatment is needed. Keep your ego in check. It is just better for everyone.

Not considering tribal members

Don't ignore family members and significant others. If they are with the patient, they are important to them and should be important to you. Patients live in an ecosystem. These people have influence over your patients and can work with you to help support your patient and improve their outcome. Make them your allies.

Not providing personalized care

Every patient has unique needs, preferences, and concerns. To avoid this, take the time to get to know your patients, provide personalized care plans, and tailor treatment options accordingly. Remember, "one size fits all" doesn't fit everyone. The cookie cutter approach is good for a factory and mass production. Not for exceptional patient care.

Not providing exceptional service

Patients expect and deserve to be treated with respect and kindness. To avoid this, provide exceptional customer service and ensure that patients are treated with the utmost care and professionalism, and work to improve your service level and, more importantly, its consistency.

Not responding to patient complaints

Be responsive and take patient complaints seriously. Investigate the problem and take steps to resolve it. Let your patients know that their complaint has been heard and what actions will be taken to improve. Express empathy for their feelings, within reason.

Not having a service recovery plan

To avoid this, have a plan in place to address and resolve any issues that arise and ensure that patients feel valued and respected. You are dealing with emotional creatures, and chances are, you are one yourself.

Not following up after the visit

Ensure that you follow up with patients after their visit to check on their well-being and ensure that any issues have been fully resolved. If you want to know if they got what they needed, well, ask!

Not providing a clean and comfortable waiting area

Ensure that the waiting area is clean, comfortable and well maintained, with comfortable seating and reading materials or entertainment available for patients. Make sure the restrooms are well maintained. This is an area that is too often neglected. Involve your entire staff in this task. Like at home, everyone is responsible, as you all live there. The "not my job" mentality has no place in an exceptional practice.

Not providing clear instructions to patients

Make sure patients receive clear instructions about follow-up care, medications, and follow-up appointments to avoid confusion and ensure proper recovery. Make sure they understand your instructions and know how to contact you if they have questions or concerns. Keep it simple and easy to remember. Provide written documentation. Use emails or text for reminders. Technology is available to you. Use it wisely.

Not providing an easy-to-use patient portal:

Make sure the patient portal is easy to use, accessible, and allows patients to access their medical records, communicate with their healthcare team, and schedule appointments. Ask for feedback and use it to optimize and always improve.

Not offering a variety of payment options:

Make it easy and convenient for them to pay you! Offer a variety of payment options to meet patients' needs and preferences. Amazon made so much headway by incorporating the "Buy with one click" option. How easy is it to pay you?

Not offering virtual consultation options

Offer virtual consultations, telemedicine, and remote monitoring services to make healthcare more accessible and convenient for patients. Patients want flexibility and convenience just like any other customer. Not offering the option today is a costly mistake.

Not being transparent about costs

Be completely transparent about costs, explain all fees and charges up front, and provide patients with a cost estimate before treatment. Make your transactions as seamless and simple as possible. Give patients peace of mind. They have enough to worry about, make sure financial terms are not one of them. People like surprises. But only the good ones.

Not providing continuity of care

Ensure that patients receive continuity of care and that their healthcare team is aware of their medical history, treatments, and follow-up appointments. The strength of a chain resides in the weakest link. Find it, and make it stronger!

Not providing a welcoming and friendly environment

A lack of friendliness and a welcoming environment can create an atmosphere of tension and fear, leading to miscommunication and misunderstanding between patients and healthcare providers. Misunderstandings can lead to misdiagnosis, a break of trust, inappropriate treatment, and medication errors. If patients do not feel comfortable or welcome in your office, they can even avoid seeking medical care altogether, which will result in delayed diagnosis and treatment of medical conditions.

Create a welcoming and friendly environment, greet patients with a smile, and ensure that staff are approachable, friendly, and willing to help with any questions or concerns. Hire front desk staff for personality and train them for skills. Medicine is a people's business.

Action Step

Pick three (or more) of the above list of things *not* to do that you know you *are* doing and list them here, along with what your strategy for turning that around.

1. _____

_____

_____

_____

2. _____

_____

_____

_____

3. _____

_____

_____

_____

IMPORTANT TIPS FOR CREATING EXCEPTIONAL PATIENT EXPERIENCES

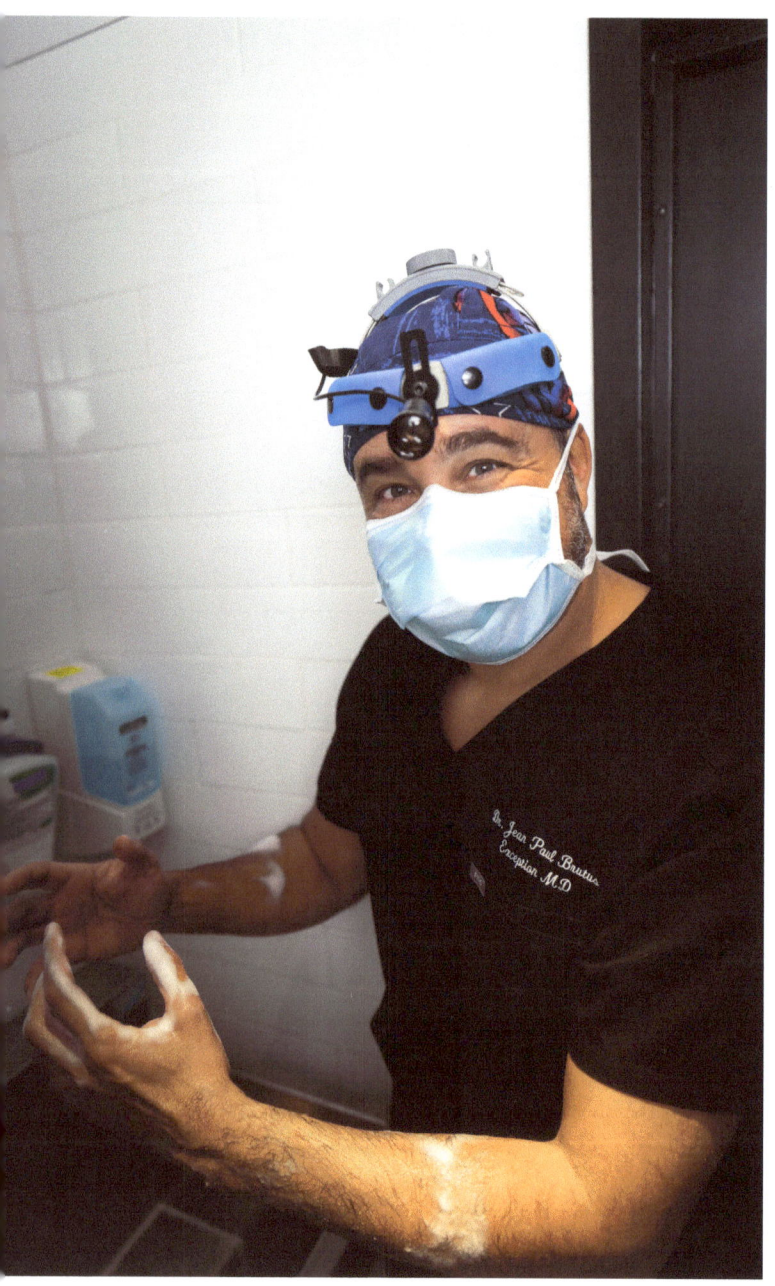
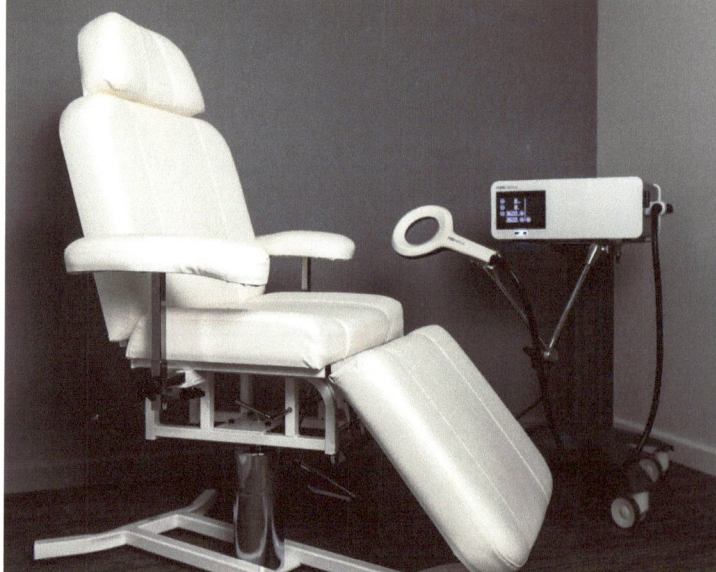

22

Prevent Burnout, Restore Joy, and Find Fulfillment

"Only a life lived in the service for others is worth living."

—ALBERT EINSTEIN

Providing quality care to your patients is a rewarding and fulfilling experience. However, the demands of the job can also lead to burnout, loss of enjoyment in your practice, and a sense of unfulfillment. Fortunately, focusing on improving the patient experience can help you prevent burnout, restore joy to your practice, and find fulfillment.

Focusing on the patient experience can be considered a kind of spiritual work because it requires a deep level of care, empathy, and understanding for the patient. It is about going beyond the physical symptoms and treating the whole person, including their emotional and spiritual needs, which are deeper aspects of the human experience. Yours too.

Spirituality is often defined as a connection to something greater than oneself, and in the context of healthcare, that connection can be made between you and your patient. When you focus on your patient experience, you are not only treating the physical symptoms, but also addressing the emotional and spiritual needs of your patient. And guess what, they are intertwined with your own. This creates a deeper level of connection and understanding between you and your patient.

Focusing on the patient experience also requires a level of selflessness and compassion. It is about putting the patient's needs and well-being ahead of your own and making sure they feel valued, respected, and understood. This selflessness and compassion are qualities often associated with spiritual practice and spiritual growth. It is about transcending self. It is about connectedness.

IMPORTANT TIPS FOR CREATING EXCEPTIONAL PATIENT EXPERIENCES

By focusing on enhancing the patient experience, you will create a deeper sense of meaning and purpose in your own life. You will connect to something greater than yourself, to the well-being of your patients, and to your connection with them.

Action Step

In what ways can you connect with yourself and your spiritual beliefs so that you can better focus on elevating your patient experience?

_____

_____

_____

_____

_____

_____

_____

_____

_____

_____

Notes

Conclusion

"The secret of change is to focus all of your energy, not on fighting the old, but on building the new."

—SOCRATES

Unhappy or frustrated patients can significantly damage the reputation of your practice, clinic, or organization by negatively advertising their experience with you. The perception patients have of service quality increasingly affects their choice of provider. Of course, by nature, perception is subjective.

Word of mouth reviews of service are becoming more and more important to the point that they matter (almost) more than your credentials and diplomas.

That is the reason my own diplomas, certifications, and awards are not displayed in my clinic or office.

Think about it. They don't represent what I am or what I do today. These credentials simply mean that once upon a time in my remote past, I did meet the criteria for certification and to be given a medical license. But what my patients think of the experience and outcomes they get with me today is far more representative of what I do today.

Do you still have the sporting medals you earned twenty years ago on your bedroom walls? I certainly hope you don't.

Prospective patients align with your WHY, not your WHAT

Each unhappy customer tells ten people about their bad experience, but one patient whose expectations were met (satisfied) but not exceeded will hardly tell anyone.

The costs associated with disappointed patients can be potentially disastrous given today's shrinking margins for healthcare providers. Focusing on patient satisfaction and experience is in line with the fundamental mission of healthcare and makes business sense.

One of the best ways to present what you do and what differentiates you from the masses is actually not putting the emphasis on WHAT you do (it still matters, of course, as we need people to do what you do) but on WHY you do it and HOW. People don't buy what you do. They buy *why* you do it. What you do just provides proof of what you believe.

Communicating your WHY will help you find the people who believe in what *you* believe in. They will be your friends, your loyal patients, and your raving fans. They will also be your best employees, teammates, and inspiring partners. You will be building a community of people who share values.

Having this type of clarity will allow you to have alignment in all that you and your practice do.

Anytime you are considering a change, doing something differently, you will be able (and well inspired) to see if it matches your WHY and HOW.

To keep it alive, your WHY will have to be communicated left, right, and center. Otherwise, and especially as you, your practice, or organization successfully grow, you (or your team) can lose sight of your WHY and HOW.

This results in decreased energy, loss of passion and drive, reduced engagement of staff and patients, and disappearance of innovation. Trust and loyalty disappear, performance bottoms out, and the end is near.

That is one of the major reasons explaining why healthcare professionals eventually burn out. They started off with an enthusiastic desire to save the world, one patient at a time, then become overwhelmed by the rigidity and resistance of the healthcare system they work in. Such healthcare systems have a huge conflict between their WHY and their WHAT and HOW.

Aren't hospitals supposed to be *hospitable*? Are they?

And yet, hospitality is in their very name.

Today, in the Western world, sadly, we have ILL-care, not healthcare.

Allow yourself to be weird and think outside the box

I mentioned earlier in this book how I turned my patient holding area into The Lounge, an environment much like a spa, and all the other little enhancements that add to the patient experience.

By doing so, I have control over their environment and their experience.

This is not just an advantage of having founded a private clinic. My colleagues, who have a private surgical facility where they provide cosmetic surgery, also have this control, but they don't do it.

Why?

They don't think of it.

I'm just weird. I don't think like a doctor.

They are normal and think like doctors; therefore, they would never even think about this.

You know what's been on my mind for the last year?

You're probably going to think I'm nuts.

In the OR, I'd like to have smoke effects, or haze effects, like you see at a concert. But I can't do this because I can't have smoke in the air when we're doing surgery.

But I'm thinking about this. *HOW* do we do this? What if there was a way?

Why?

Because it's an experience.

Remember, this is the conversation (or similar) both you and the patient want:

Patient: "Oh! Wait, surgery's done?"

Me: "Yeah!"

Patient: "I never even felt it."

Me: "I know."

That is magic. Provide the magic.

You don't need the fog machine.

You don't even need laser shows or playlists. But you can!

You don't have to make it a miserable experience.

There are things you can do to make it pleasant.

If you've read this far and you're not sold on the idea yet, look at your iPad. Before the iPad existed, I couldn't sell you on the idea of one. We couldn't conceive of it. But once the first iPad was out, a lot of people said, "I *want* this!"

As Apple co-founder Steve Jobs said, don't ask people what they want. They have no idea. *You* have to create it first. Then they'll want it.

He's right. He was that type of thinker. He was able to see the invisible, what didn't exist, and he knew that when people would see it too, they'd go berserk.

Other people have this talent. Warren Buffett sees it with financials. You can't see what he sees, and I can't see what he sees. That's why he's where he is. He's got this vision. Jeff Bezos had a vision for Amazon that no one else had. No one thought it would ever work. He started with books, but it was The Everything Store that he wanted. That's pretty much what it is today.

Are you able to see what others in your field can't yet see?

If so, then you have the power to elevate your patients' experience.

There's a lot that *you* can do that everyone else is not doing—even those who have control. They won't do it if it doesn't bring them a benefit, which is either money or happiness, or ideally both.

But you can't be against what's good.

You can't be against a pleasant or elevated patient experience.

It will benefit you, your bottom line, and you will end up enjoying the feeling of creating an amazing experience. It will delight your patients, who will regard you as the one who made their day, or changed their life for the better.

Know why this matters to you. Know why this matters to your patients.

Now go do it.

Just a little bit.

Then a little bit more.

CONCLUSION

Action Steps

Ideal patients want to connect with your WHY. Having read this book, what's yours?

_____

_____

_____

_____

What's the weirdest thing you can think of that would enhance your facility or patient experience? Allow yourself to go really weird. How would you go about it?

_____

_____

_____

_____

What's the first thing you'll do after finishing this book to elevate your patient experience?

_____

_____

_____

_____

Notes

Acknowledgments

Writing this book was a journey that would not have been possible without the unwavering support, dedication, and expertise of a remarkable team of individuals. Their commitment to creating an exceptional patient experience has not only shaped the content of this book, but has also changed the lives of countless patients. I am deeply grateful to each of them for their contributions and unwavering support.

Stephanie, your organizational skills, your sixth sense, and problem-solving abilities are truly extraordinary. Your innovative ideas have left an indelible mark on our journey. Your homemade brownies, cookies, and cupcakes have brought comfort to all our patients after surgery and put a smile on their face.

Kira, your attention to detail and creative approach to improving the patient experience have raised the bar in our practice. Your ability to ease patients and your compassion are invaluable.

Thien, your unwavering commitment to excellence and your ability to lead by example have been a driving force behind our success. Your leadership has inspired all of us to strive for greatness.

Patricia, your warmth, empathy, and genuine connections with patients have had a profound impact. Your ability to reassure our patients at ease is a gift we all admire.

Christiane, your organizational skills and ability to keep our operations running smoothly have been instrumental in providing a seamless patient experience. Your efforts behind the scenes do not go unnoticed.

Nicolas, your technical expertise and availability are essential to our ability to provide world-class care.

Thank you, Roxie, for brightening up our environment with your smile and keeping our patients safe.

To my extraordinary team, you are the heart and soul of our mission to provide an exceptional patient experience. This book is a tribute to your hard work, dedication, and unwavering commitment to making a difference in the lives of our patients. Thank you for being an integral part of this journey.

About the Author

Dr. Jean-Paul Brutus is a plastic and reconstructive surgeon specializing in minimally invasive hand surgery. He trained in Belgium, Canada, and the United States. With more than twenty years of experience in hand surgery, Dr. Brutus has taught hand surgery skills to plastic surgeons, orthopedic surgeons, physiatrists, physical therapists, and occupational therapists around the world.

After an academic practice as adjunct professor in reconstructive plastic and hand surgery in one of the largest teaching hospitals in Canada, he co-founded Exception MD, a private clinic in Montreal entirely devoted to upper and lower extremity orthopedic surgery.

Dr. Brutus is passionate about two things: state-of-the-art minimally invasive hand surgery and patient experience.

Inspired by leaders in the service and hospitality industries, he is committed to raising the standards in healthcare, not just for the quality of the care, but also in the quality of the caring and in the patient's experience.

He believes surgery does not have to be a traumatic experience.

Nobody wants to have surgery, but patients do want a positive outcome. With surgeons who meet the patient's physical and emotional needs, the experience of surgery can be transformed completely for the benefit of all.

Connect with Dr. Brutus:

Facebook @Dr.Brutus
Instagram @dr.brutus
YouTube @drbrutuschannel
LinkedIn @jean-paul-brutus-md-3b365819
Webpage http://www.drbrutus.com

Please Consider Donating

Thank you for reading this book!

By buying this book, you have helped to contribute proceeds to Welcome Hall Mission, a vital organization here in Montreal that helps families in need, at-risk mothers and youth, and those experiencing homelessness.

Welcome Hall Mission is near and dear to my heart. I began volunteering at its food bank many years ago and soon brought my surgeon colleagues to help, too. At a time when contributing to the community was not considered an important lesson for medical students, the director of the local medical school saw what my colleagues and I were doing, and integrated that activity into her program.

If you feel called to donate more to Welcome Hall Mission, you may do so on their webpage.

http://welcomehallmission.com/donate

Thank you.
Dr. JeanPaul Brutus

Other Books by Dr. Jean-Paul Brutus

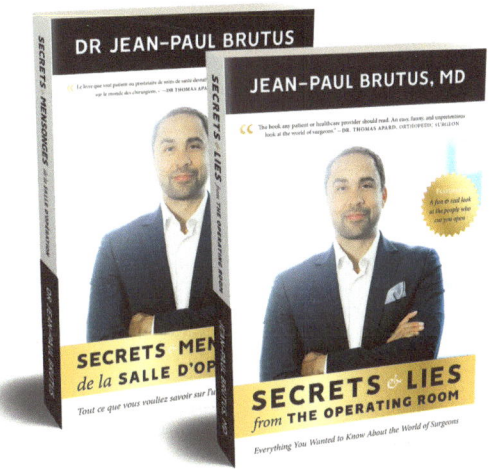

SECRETS AND LIES FROM THE OPERATING ROOM

Learn the secrets of the surgical world, without going to medical school!

For millions of people, having surgery is a confounding, uncomfortable, and even fearful experience. In *Secrets and Lies from the Operating Room,* Dr. Jean-Paul Brutus separates fact from fallacy and tells you everything you need to know about the world of surgeons.

HELPING HANDS

In addition to his medical career, Dr. Brutus is an active philanthropist. Among other initiatives, he compiled and published *Tendre la main,* a unique photography book that depicts hands as tools for helping others. The proceeds from the sale of the book, which was created with the voluntary contribution of twelve renowned photographers and over forty Québec personalities, were donated to la Fondation Les Impatients to support mental health and artistic expression.

www.ingramcontent.com/pod-product-compliance
Lightning Source LLC
LaVergne TN
LVHW070612080526
838200LV00103B/348